What is psychology?

Third edition:

> I could not ask for a better introduction for students intending to study psychology.
>
> Nicky Hayes, Visiting Senior Fellow, University of Surrey

Comments on the previous editions:

> It is done with panache, with unusual and vivid examples, and
> ~~with clarity. It ~~ ... ~~our~~ of psychology

... *hological Reviews*

... and the amateur
... y is really about.
... rzillier in *Changes*

... sumes no prior
... dated, this third
... sities. Examples
... as, with a self-
... er of intriguing
... chology, psychi-
... professions and
... Suggestions for

... e University of
... us publications
... 994) and *Game*
... *sciences* (1995).

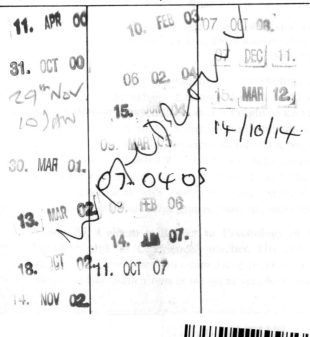

What is psychology?
Third edition

Andrew M. Colman

Illustrated by Angela Chorley

London and New York

First published 1981 by Kogan Page Ltd
Second edition published 1988 by Hutchinson Education

Third edition first published 1999
by Routledge
11 New Fetter Lane, London EC4P 4EE

Routledge is an imprint of the Taylor & Francis Group

Simultaneously published in the USA and Canada
by Routledge
29 West 35th Street, New York, NY 10001

© 1981, 1988, 1999 Andrew M. Colman
Illustrations © 1999 Angela Chorley

Typeset in Times by Routledge
Printed and bound in Great Britain by
Biddles Ltd, Guildford and King's Lynn

British Library Cataloguing in Publication Data
A catalogue record for this book is available from the British
Library

Library of Congress Cataloging in Publication Data
Colman, Andrew M.
   What is psychology? / Andrew M. Colman. – 3rd ed.
   Includes bibliographical references and index.
   1. Psychology. 1. Title.
BF121.C595   1999
150–dc21   98–31960

ISBN 0–415–16901–1 (hbk)
ISBN 0–415–16902–x (pbk)

Contents

Preface

This is an updated and considerably improved version of the book. The second edition remained steadily in demand for a decade, but during that time psychology and the world moved on and the need for a new edition gradually increased until it could no longer be ignored. The publisher eventually asked me for a third edition, and my literary agent gently but firmly prodded me into writing it. I used the opportunity to make numerous improvements, both large and small.

The subtitle that was appended to the second edition has been dropped, because the reason for it – another book with the same title – has disappeared. Almost every chapter has been thoroughly rewritten. The bibliographic references have been substantially extended and updated, and I have tried wherever possible to include the best of the most recent publications. I have occasionally cited Internet web sites in addition to books and articles, especially in chapter 6 where readers need the latest information about training and careers, but also to a lesser extent elsewhere in the book.

I have improved and tidied up chapters 1 and 2, but I have refrained from changing the questions in the self-assessment quiz in chapter 2, although I have thoroughly updated the explanations of the answers. One reason for keeping the original questions is that researchers have used the quiz to test the knowledge of prospective students of psychology and have published the results, and these normative data have enabled me to recalibrate the interpretation of scores on the basis of something slightly more solid than inspired guesswork.

In chapter 3, devoted to the subject matter of psychology, I have had to revise the content substantially in the light of recent developments. It is (once again) surprising how quickly psychology has changed – each time I revise this book I feel like exclaiming, "My, how you've grown!'". I have introduced material on cognitive neuropsychology, new techniques of brain imaging, and cognitive research into imagery; I have updated the discussion of artificial intelligence to incorporate computational and connectionist models, and I have beefed up the discussion of mental disorders to bring it into line with the current terminology of the latest edition of the American Psychiatric Association's *Diagnostic and Statistical Manual of Mental Disorders* (*DSM-IV*); and I have introduced numerous other rejuvenations. I have radically restructured the discussion of research methods in chapter 4, separating correlational studies from quasi-experiments and adding brief discussions of qualitative research methods and multiple regression techniques to reflect changing fashions in psychological research. I have slightly improved chapter 5, on the history of psychology, and have added the dates of historical personalities to provide a more precise sense of time. I have had to make substantial changes to chapter 6, on the professions of psychology, to reflect changes affecting clinical psychology, counselling psychology, and above all forensic and criminological psychology, and to take account of emerging professions of health psychology and sports psychology. I have made numerous other improvements, both cosmetic and substantive, throughout the book.

The cartoons used in the first and second editions were drawn almost 30 years ago and were beginning to show their age. I am delighted that the original artist Angela Chorley was willing to create a new set of cartoons for this edition.

Andrew M. Colman

Preface to the second edition

The first edition of this book received favourable comments from reviewers and general readers, and even elicited the sincerest form of flattery – another book with the identical title, which appeared in 1985. To avoid confusion I have added a distinctive subtitle to this second edition.

The book is designed for general readers who want to know what psychology is all about. It is suitable for people who are considering studying psychology at universities, polytechnics, and colleges but are not sure what they would be letting themselves in for. It has also been used in adult education classes and as a first introduction for A level and degree students.

Every chapter has been thoroughly revised. Numerous minor amendments and improvements have been made, suggestions for further reading have been updated, and the final chapter has been altered to reflect changes in professional psychology since the publication of the first edition. The self-assessment quiz, which everyone seems to have liked, has been rewritten and generally tidied up, and a few of the original questions have been replaced by better ones.

The first edition included a long chapter in which the logic of statistics was explained from first principles through the laborious analysis of a specific numerical example. I am now convinced that this ambitious experiment was misguided. Non-mathematical readers simply skipped the chapter, and readers with some mathematical background found the detailed explanations of every little step in the argument tiresome and unnecessary; neither group could see the wood for the trees. I am reminded of the anxious mother who made her son promise, when he joined the air force, that he would always fly slowly and as close to the ground as possible. I have therefore considerably condensed the section on statistics and placed it more logically alongside the discussion of research methods in chapter 4.

In addition to the people who helped me with the first edition, I should like to thank Michael Argyle, Sarah Conibear, Alison Dunbar-Dempsey, Rosemary Duxbury, Susan Dye, Brian Foss, Robert Hemmings, Eric Liknaitzky, Andrew Mayes, John Radford, and Bill Williamson.

A.M.C.
March 1988

Preface to the first edition

This book is written primarily for seriously interested members of the general public and intending students of psychology. With such readers in mind, I have tried to convey a vivid and realistic picture of the subject as it is taught in colleges and universities and of the activities of professional psychologists in their various fields of employment.

I have departed in two important ways from the usual conventions of brief introductory books. The first is a matter of style. I have made copious use of concrete examples, given in sufficient detail to enable the reader to grasp them "in the round" rather than merely to glimpse them in silhouette. These examples are intended to illustrate psychological research methods and findings and, more important, to provide a framework for discussing the ideas that lie behind them. The emphasis is always on discussion and explanation rather than bare description, and the reader is encouraged to take nothing for granted.

The second unusual feature of this book concerns its subject matter. I have included certain interesting and important topics that are dealt with in all undergraduate courses but are generally neglected or mentioned without explanation in books intended for non-psychologists. These are matters that bewilder most people and frighten intending students. For example, research methods and statistics are discussed at some length because they are of central importance to most areas of psychology and are part of the core curriculum of all reputable degree courses. Since brief, non-technical accounts are not readily available elsewhere, I have grasped the nettle and tried to present the essential ideas in a way that even the most non-mathematical readers should find palatable. I have included also a chapter on the history of psychology, in the belief that ideas are often easier to understand when they are viewed in historical perspective, and also because the development of psychology as a science is a fascinating subject in itself.

This is not a textbook. I have made no attempt to provide a balanced survey of the entire field of psychology, because any such attempt would be vain in a volume of this size and would, in any case, frustrate its essential aims. There are several excellent textbooks available; some of them are referred to in the pages that follow. I have concentrated instead on trying to convey the flavour of the subject through a selection of its most important problems, methods and findings. It is inevitable that some psychologists will not share my judgement of what is most important, and others will no doubt take issue with some of the opinions I express: psychology is a controversial subject.

A number of friends and colleagues examined parts of an earlier draft of this book and made helpful comments. The following, in particular, brought grist to my mill: Felicity Dirmeick, Peter Freeman, Julia Gibbs, Gabriele Griffin, Ian Pountney, Jane Simpson, and Robert Thomson. Thanks are due also to Katy Carter of Kogan Page, who suggested a number of improvements, to Angela Chorley, who produced the captivating cartoons, and to Dorothy Brydges, who typed the manuscript.

A.M.C.
July 1980

Chapter 1

Getting started

O latest born and loveliest vision far
Of all Olympus' faded hierarchy

Keats, "Ode to Psyche"

Definitions

Psychology is a popular and rapidly growing subject. Among all the major branches of knowledge, it has the curious distinction of being the one that is most often misspelt. This is often harmless enough, but it can sometimes cause problems. If you try to look up psychology in a dictionary but are not sure how to spell it, you might end up reading a definition of phycology (the study of algae), physiology (the study of biological processes in plants and animals), psephology (the statistical and sociological study of elections), psychography (spirit-writing), or even pseudology (the art or science of lying). If you can spell psychology, you already know more about it than many people do.

The word *psychology* first appeared in English in 1693 but was not widely used or understood until the mid 1800s. It was coined by joining together the Greek words *psyche* and *logos*. *Psyche* originally meant breath, but it later came to mean soul as well, because breathing was thought to indicate that the soul had not yet left the body. In Greek mythology, the soul was personified by Psyche (with a capital P), a young woman who was loved by Eros, the god of love. Eros married Psyche but visited her only at night and insisted that she should never see his face, but one night her curiosity overcame her and she lit an oil lamp while he was asleep. She fell in love with Eros at first sight but was so startled by his beauty that she spilt a drop of hot oil on his shoulder and awakened him, and when

he realized what she had done he abandoned her. To win him back, Psyche had to endure many trials and dangers, but eventually she was transformed into a goddess and joined him in heavenly bliss. This explains why Psyche is often depicted in works of art with butterfly wings or as a butterfly. Psyche symbolizes the human soul, suffering hardship and struggle in life but re-emerging after death in a new and better existence, like a caterpillar reborn as a butterfly.

During the seventeenth century, the meaning of the Greek word *psyche* broadened to include mind. *Logos*, the other Greek word from which *psychology* was formed, originally meant word and later came to mean discourse or reason. According to its Greek roots, therefore, psychology is literally discourse or reasoning about the mind, or as we would say today, the study of the mind, and that is the definition to be found in some dictionaries.

That definition seems straightforward and natural, but it is unsatisfactory for two main reasons. First, contemporary psychology is concerned not only with inner mental processes but also with outward behaviour. Psychologists even study brain mechanisms, many of which are only indirectly related to mental processes, and such things as reflexes and instincts that have next to nothing to do with the mind in the ordinary sense of the word. Second, philosophers have argued that anyone who believes that the mind exists independently of the body – that there is a ghost in the machine – is committing a category mistake based on the fallacy of mind–body dualism. A category mistake is a statement or belief about something belonging to one category that is intelligible only in relation to something belonging to another. According to this view, a belief that the mind can exist independently of physical behaviour is a category mistake, as is a belief that a team spirit can exist independently of the team members, or that a grin can exist independently of a face or body, as happens near the end of chapter 6 of *Alice's Adventures in Wonderland* by Lewis Carroll, when the Cheshire Cat "vanished quite slowly, beginning with the end of the tail, and ending with the grin, which remained some time after the rest of it had gone".

For these reasons, many contemporary psychologists prefer to define psychology as *the study of behaviour* or *the science of behaviour*. But these definitions raise problems of their own. Although it is true that psychologists base most of their research findings on observations of behaviour, they are often interested in the unobservable mental processes underlying the behaviour rather than the behaviour itself. To clarify this point, let me give you an example from the study of dreaming (there will be more about dreams in chapter 2). When psychologists study dreaming, they observe various physical processes, including rapid eye movements, deep muscular relaxation, characteristic patterns of brain waves, and (in male dreamers) penile erections. We know that these are signs of dreaming because if we wake people up when they are showing them they tell us that they were dreaming, whereas if we wake them at other times they do not. But the physiological signs are of no great psychological interest in themselves; their significance lies in the fact that they are associated with the mental experience of dreaming.

In other words, the trouble with the fashionable definitions of psychology as the study of behaviour or the science of behaviour is that they can be misleading. Psychologists often study aspects of behaviour only in order to make inferences about underlying thoughts and feelings, and if these inferences were not possible, then the whole justification of the research would collapse. There are even some mental processes, such as thinking and remembering, that are studied by psychologists in spite of the fact that they are not necessarily accompanied by *any* observable behaviour. It is quite possible to sit quietly in a corner and think about or remember something without batting an eyelid, and indirect research methods are needed to study such phenomena. It is worth pointing out that indirect methods are accepted without fuss in other sciences. For example, astronomers study many things that cannot be observed directly. In addition to optical images, they routinely analyse X-ray, infra-red, and radio emissions from objects in space. But it would be silly to define astronomy as the study of electromagnetic signals from space, as if the signals themselves rather than the objects and events that they signify were the focus of interest. For the same reason, it seems slightly perverse to define psychology as the study or science of behaviour, as if psychologists were interested only in outward behaviour, and never in the mental experiences that are often associated with it.

The upshot of all this is that there is no generally accepted definition of psychology. But a book should deliver what its title promises, and authors should not shirk their responsibilities, so here is the definition that I think is best, all things considered: *psychology is the science of the nature, functions, and phenomena of behaviour and mental experience*. Underlying this definition is the fundamental assumption that behaviour and mental experience are governed by rational laws that we can discover and understand, and some of the evidence in support of that assumption will emerge in later chapters. There are objections that could be raised against this definition of psychology, but nothing would be gained by prolonging the discussion because it is impossible to give a definition that would solve all the problems and satisfy everyone. Quibbles about the precise meanings of words are nearly always a waste of time (except in courts of law, where they can be highly profitable or extremely costly), and it is a mistake to think that to know how something is defined is to understand it. The best way to gain an understanding of psychology is by looking at examples of the kinds of things psychologists do and the kinds of things they regard as falling outside the boundaries of their subject. Chapter 2 contains many examples of the first kind, but let me first mention some of the things that are often mistaken for psychology.

What psychology is not

Psychology is often confused with other academic subjects, practices, and professions. I shall discuss a few of the more common cases of mistaken identity. This will achieve the twin goals of helping to fix the boundaries of psychology and eliminating several popular fallacies.

1 *Psychiatry*   This is a branch of medicine concerned with the

nature, causes, diagnosis, treatment, and prevention of mental disorders. A psychiatrist is a medical practitioner who has undergone a conventional medical training before specializing in psychiatry rather than, for instance, gynaecology, cardiology, general practice, or any other branch of medicine. As a medical specialist, a psychiatrist treats psychiatric patients in hospitals and cases referred by general practitioners.

What is the difference between psychology and psychiatry? Psychologists are not medically trained; their entire professional training is devoted to psychology. Furthermore, the work that most psychologists do has little or nothing to do with mental disorders, because psychology is concerned mainly with normal behaviour and mental experience. But the picture is complicated by the existence of a profession called clinical psychology, which I shall discuss in chapter 6. A significant proportion of psychologists belong to this profession. Clinical psychologists treat mentally disordered patients in psychiatric hospitals and elsewhere, and to that extent their work resembles psychiatry. A patient receiving treatment for a mental disorder may be forgiven for not realizing that Dr Tweedledum (MB, Ch.B., DPM) is a medical practitioner with a diploma in psychological medicine, in other words a psychiatrist, whereas Dr Tweedledee (B.Sc., M.Sc., Ph.D.) is a clinical psychologist who happens to have a doctoral degree in psychology but is not medically trained. The patient may, however, notice certain differences in the psychiatrist's and the psychologist's approach to treatment. Dr Tweedledee, the clinical psychologist, will not prescribe medical forms of treatment such as drugs, ECT (electro-convulsive therapy, or shock treatment), or psychosurgery.

2 *Psychoanalysis*   This is a theory of mental structure and function, or more correctly a loosely connected set of theories and propositions, and an associated method of psychotherapy based on the writings of the Austrian physician Sigmund Freud (1856–1939). Its distinctive character lies in the emphasis that Freud placed on unconscious mental processes and the various mechanisms people use to repress them. A familiar example is the Oedipus complex. Most psychoanalysts believe that pre-adolescent boys develop this complex as a result of repressing sexual desire for their mothers and jealousy of their fathers, and that girls develop a mirror-image complex called the Electra complex. Some people find this theory hard to swallow, but there are other aspects of psychoanalytic

theory that are far more plausible. In chapter 4 I shall discuss a brilliant example of psychoanalytic theorizing to explain a mystery surrounding a fairly common mental disorder.

As a therapeutic method, psychoanalysis relies on four main techniques designed to throw light on unconscious mental processes. The first is called *free association*. Psychoanalysts try to create an accepting and non-threatening atmosphere to pacify their clients' psychological defences, and they then encourage their clients to relate whatever comes to mind, without hesitation or censorship, however trivial or embarrassing some of the thoughts and feelings might seem.

The second technique is *dream analysis*. With the help of free association, psychoanalysts help their clients to interpret the symbolic meaning of their dreams. According to psychoanalytic theory, the latent content of all dreams consists of unconscious wish-fulfilments, which are potentially disturbing to the dreamer and would interrupt sleep if they were not disguised through symbolism.

A third technique is the analysis of *parapraxes*, or to use a more familiar term, Freudian slips. Psychoanalysts believe in the law of psychic determinism, according to which all behaviour is the result of psychological motives that are sometimes unconscious, and they also believe that this law applies not only to deliberate actions but also to slips of the tongue and other apparently accidental actions. Parapraxes are analysed for possible clues to repressed thoughts and desires by a method similar to dream analysis.

The last of the main psychoanalytic techniques is the analysis of the *transference*. The transference is a dependent, child-like, and often sexually charged relationship that a person undergoing psychoanalysis usually forms with the analyst, and this relationship is likely to have features carried over (transferred) from earlier relationships, especially with parents. Psychoanalysts believe that the transference provides a context in which aspects of past relationships can be usefully explored.

A full psychoanalysis is a lengthy (and costly) affair involving several 50-minute sessions per week over a period of years. The ultimate goal of the analysis is to identify repressed thoughts and feelings, to understand the reasons for their repression, and to learn to accept them consciously and rationally.

Since the early decades of this century when Freud was practising, the psychoanalytic movement has been riven by doctrinal conflicts. The most influential contemporary schools are based on the writings of Sigmund's daughter Anna Freud (1895–1982), the Austrian-born British psychoanalyst Melanie Klein (1882–1960), the Swiss psychoanalyst Carl Gustav Jung (1875–1961), and the Austrian psychoanalyst Alfred Adler (1870–1937). Their followers call themselves Freudian, Kleinian, Jungian, and Adlerian analysts respectively. The Jungian and Adlerian schools, in particular, represent radical departures from the original theories and methods of Sigmund Freud.

The interrelationships between psychoanalysis, psychology, and psychiatry are quite confusing. Psychoanalysts are not necessarily qualified in psychology or psychiatry – their essential training involves undergoing psychoanalysis themselves – but some psychologists and psychiatrists do become psychoanalysts. A further source of confusion is the fact that, especially in continental Europe and parts of the Third World, many psychologists and psychiatrists who are not qualified psychoanalysts are more or less psychoanalytically inclined in their approach. On the other hand, in the United Kingdom, the United States, and other English-speaking countries most psychologists hold views that are distinctly non-psychoanalytic or even hostile to psychoanalysis.

3 *Psychometrics* Roughly speaking, psychometrics is mental testing. It includes IQ testing, ability and aptitude testing, and the use of psychological tests for measuring interests, attitudes, and personality traits or mental disorders. The history of psychometrics can be traced to 1905, when Alfred Binet (1857–1911) and Théodore Simon (1873–1961) developed the world's first standardized intelligence test in France. Psychometrics soon became an integral part of psychology, particularly of those areas of psychology that are concerned with individual differences and personality, to be outlined in chapter 3. But most areas of contemporary psychology make no use of psychometrics because they deal with general psychological processes rather than individual differences. In spite of this fact, some people erroneously identify psychometrics with psychology as a whole, probably because the

only direct contact that many people have with psychology involves mental testing at school.

People are often disturbed, and also sceptical, about the possibility of expressing their quintessentially human qualities, such as their intelligence or personality, in the form of mere numbers. Doubts of this kind usually arise from a misunderstanding of the logic of measurement, and they are on the whole not shared by people who have studied psychology. But criticisms of the uses to which psychometrics has sometimes been put cannot be dismissed so easily. Many psychologists admit that IQ tests in particular have often been abused for social and political purposes. For example, the importation of the Binet-Simon IQ test into the United States contributed to the enactment of sterilization laws designed to prevent "subnormals", criminals, and other deviant groups from reproducing. Also in the United States, the blatantly racist Immigration Restriction Act of 1924 that prevented hundreds of thousands of Jewish refugees from escaping the Nazi Holocaust was given pseudo-scientific respectability by psychometric surveys purporting to show that central and eastern Europeans had low IQs. In the United Kingdom, the Education Act of 1944 introduced the divisive eleven-plus examination, based largely on IQ tests, and for more than a generation children who failed it were denied entry to the grammar schools that prepared pupils for higher education and were sent instead to academically inferior secondary modern schools, where they remained even if their intellectual or scholastic ability improved dramatically in later years.

4 Philosophy A rough-and-ready definition of philosophy is "thought about thought". Many of the issues that non-psychologists assume to be part of psychology are really philosophical problems. These are questions that cannot be settled by any imaginable observations of behaviour but by their nature must be dealt with by rational argument alone. Let me illustrate this distinction with a few examples.

The psychology of perception (several aspects of which will be discussed in chapters 2 and 3) is devoted to investigating how people gain information about their environment through their sense organs. A major branch of philosophy, called epistemology, also focuses on how people learn about the world, but it deals with quite different types of questions. For example, one of the central problems of epistemology is the problem of induction, first formulated by the Scottish philosopher David Hume (1711–1776) in the eighteenth century. The problem is this: how can we reach general conclusions about the world on the basis of particular observations? How can we justify the *general* conclusion that apples fall to the ground when released, when all we really know is that *particular* apples that we have observed have fallen? If induction from particular observations to general laws is not rationally defensible, as philosophers since Hume have had to admit, then how is science possible, bearing in mind that scientists can make only particular observations? It is futile (though tempting) to argue that the many obvious successes of science prove that induction works, because that argument is itself inductive. How can we know that science works in general when we have seen it working only in particular instances? It is clear that we cannot solve the problem of induction, or contribute anything to it for that matter, by studying behaviour and mental experience, therefore it cannot be a psychological problem. It is an irreducibly philosophical problem, which can be tackled only by rational argument.

Consider next the issue of morality. Psychologists investigate the development and nature of moral attitudes by studying the responses of children and adults to ethical dilemmas, and intriguing findings occasionally emerge from this research. For example, the Swiss psychologist Jean Piaget (1896–1980) carried out an experiment in which children aged 5 years and 10 years were told two stories. In one story, a boy breaks fifteen cups by accident, and in the second a boy breaks one cup while trying to steal jam from a cupboard. When Piaget asked the children which boy was naughtier, most of the 5-year-old children replied that the boy who broke fifteen cups was naughtier, and most of the 10-year-old children replied that the boy who broke one cup while stealing was naughtier. Piaget was testing the hypothesis that children below 7 years measure the morality of an action by the amount of harm done and older children by the motive or intention behind the action. But there are problems of morality that cannot be approached in this way because of their essentially philosophical character. Such problems are dealt with in the branch of philosophy called ethics. For example, the sentence "It is wrong to tell lies" seems from its grammatical form to be a factual statement, and therefore it ought to be either true or false, but how could it ever be verified or refuted? Is it possible, either by logical argument or factual evidence, to decide whether a moral utterance is true or false? Or is it a fallacy – a version of what philosophers call the naturalistic fallacy – to believe that it is a factual statement? In that case, does it mean anything, and if so what does it mean? Like the problem of induction that I discussed earlier, and for the same reason, these are purely philosophical problems.

I ought to mention two rather trivial sources of confusion about philosophy and psychology. First, there is a small field of psychological research, called philosophical psychology, devoted to the interface between the two disciplines. It deals with philosophical problems that are relevant to psychology and psychological problems that are relevant to philosophy. Second, many psychologists who have never studied philosophy hold the degree of Doctor of Philosophy (Ph.D. or D.Phil.). The doctoral degree that is awarded for advanced postgraduate research, not only in philosophy but also in psychology and most other subjects, is a doctorate of philosophy. For strange and obscure historical reasons, medical practitioners are allowed to call themselves doctors even if they do not have doctoral degrees. This anomaly arose in the eighteenth century. In Samuel Johnson's *Dictionary*, published in 1755, the primary meaning of *doctor* (which comes from Latin *docere*, to teach) was still someone holding a higher degree and thus competent to teach a subject or expound on a field of knowledge, but by that time medical practitioners were already beginning to usurp the word to describe themselves, whether or not they held such qualifications, and although there were objections from people with legitimate doctorates, by the end of the century this practice had become commonplace. The medical profession apparently purloined the title. Nowadays one even hears of people with doctorates being accused of not being real doctors because they are not medically qualified, and the irony is not usually intentional.

5 *Parapsychology*   This is a minor field of psychological research devoted to investigating allegedly paranormal (beyond the normal) phenomena. The two classes of paranormal phenomena that have been most thoroughly studied are extra-sensory perception (ESP) and psychokinesis (PK). ESP is defined as perception without the use of sense organs, and it includes telepathy (extra-sensory perception of other people's mental processes, or in more familiar language mind-reading) and clairvoyance (extra-sensory perception of physical objects or events). Precognitive telepathy or clairvoyance, or simply precognition, is defined as extra-sensory perception

of events in the future. PK or psychokinesis (from Greek *psyche*, mind + *kinesis*, movement) is defined as the movement or change of physical objects by mental processes without the application of physical force.

Parapsychology has a long history, and a lot of painstaking research has gone into trying to find evidence for ESP in particular. Opinion surveys have repeatedly shown that a majority of ordinary people believe in ESP, but that scientists tend to be sceptical about it and psychologists especially so. Parapsychologists believe that there is convincing scientific evidence that ESP occurs, and they sometimes accuse sceptical scientists of burying their heads in the sand and deliberately ignoring or suppressing this evidence because it challenges conventional theories and beliefs. The sceptics claim that the evidence is quite inconclusive for several reasons. First, although parapsychologists have often reported positive results, no one has found a repeatable experiment or procedure that always, or even usually, produces positive results when sceptical experimenters perform it. Second, many of the research findings that parapsychologists have regarded as convincing evidence of the paranormal have turned out to be false dawns arising from flawed experiments or, in numerous cases, fraud or deception by the participants (subjects) or experimenters. Third, paranormal phenomena are by definition so extraordinary that extraordinarily strong evidence is needed to establish their reality, but the existing evidence is equivocal at best, and certainly not strong enough to convince a hardened sceptic. The last and most fundamental criticism arises from the fact that paranormal phenomena are defined negatively, as events that have no normal explanation. The problem is that any putatively paranormal phenomenon may have some perfectly normal explanation that has been overlooked or has yet to be discovered, and if such a normal explanation were revealed, then the phenomenon could no longer be called paranormal. Eclipses, comets, volcanic eruptions, and plague epidemics were all attributed to supernatural causes before they were properly understood as natural phenomena.

Sceptics claim that it is impossible to prove that a phenomenon is paranormal, because no one could ever be sure that all possible normal explanations had been ruled out. But ways have often been found to do things that were once considered impossible. Who would have believed, as recently as a century ago, that we would one day be able to sit in our living-rooms and watch a football match as it was being played on the other side of the world? And is it fair to expect higher standards of proof in parapsychology than in any other field of psychological research? Most parapsychologists are unimpressed with the sceptical arguments. Parapsychology is a small but active field of research involving investigators from several disciplines. Many of the researchers in this area are psychologists, but it is also true to say that the concerns of most psychologists are far removed from parapsychology.

6 Sociology This word was invented by the nineteenth-century French philosopher and mathematician Auguste Comte (1798–1857) as a label for the study of human societies and the structures and processes within them. The writings of three influential social theorists have shaped its development. The German political philosopher Karl Marx (1818–1883) argued that economic modes and relations of production are the fundamental bases of the structures and ideologies within all societies, and he drew particular attention to the importance of class conflict in the functioning and change of societies. The French sociologist Émile Durkheim (1858–1917) challenged the assumption that social processes can be understood in terms of the actions of individuals and argued that even suicide, apparently the ultimately individualistic act, cannot be fully explained at the purely individual level. Durkheim used survey data to show that egoistic suicide (which is more common among single than married people) arises from a lack of social cohesion, altruistic suicide (relatively common in Japan) from a sense of failure to society, and anomic suicide (rare among Catholics) from an absence of social norms that he called *anomie*. The German economist and sociologist Max Weber (1864–1920) focused attention on the social implications of rationality, interpreting economics and law as forms of rational human action and religion as a model of non-rational action, and he classified types of authority and bureaucracy according to this distinction.

There are clearly areas of overlap between sociology and psychology, an obvious example being social attitudes, which are studied in both disciplines. But the two disciplines tend to approach their subject matter at different levels, even when they deal with the same phenomena. Sociologists study societies and social processes and are not primarily in the business of investigating or explaining individual human behaviour, whereas psychologists tend to study social phenomena only in so far as they help to explain individual or at least small-group behaviour. A more fundamental difference between the two disciplines relates to research methods. Psychologists rely heavily on experimental evidence to test their theories (there will be more about research methods in chapter 4). Sociologists also rely on evidence, usually from surveys, but they cannot usually carry out controlled experiments because of the nature of their subject matter.

One of the major areas of psychological research is social psychology, and this is also on the syllabus of degree courses in sociology. Students are occasionally confused by the fact that there is a subtle difference between the psychological and sociological versions of social psychology. Different textbooks tend to be used, and the sociological version of social psychology is noticeably different in flavour from the version taught to psychology students. Experimental social psychology, in particular, is often treated with disdain (and incomprehension) by sociologists.

Studying psychology

The discussion of definitions at the beginning of this chapter provides one kind of answer to the question in the book's title, but a definition conveys scarcely anything of the flavour of a subject. The discussion about what psychology is *not* should have inoculated you against some of the fallacies that abound in newspapers, films, television programmes, novels, popular magazines, and everyday conversations. Psychologists wince whenever people mistake them for psychiatrists, or ask them at parties whether they are psychoanalysing the guests, or complain to them about their children's grossly unfair IQ scores, or expect them to engage in deep philosophical discussions about the morality of abortion, or to express an expert opinion on telepathy, or to comment weightily on social problems. Psychologists are constantly subjected to these and similar provocations, and the popular myth that psychologists tend to be mentally unbalanced would have a convenient explanation if it were true – in fact, research has shown that we are no different from other professional groups in this respect.

Having read as far as this, you will probably avoid falling into the usual traps. But the only way to achieve anything approaching a proper understanding of psychology is by examining some of the fine detail of the subject from close range. There are no short cuts to understanding an established academic discipline. The best way to study psychology is to enrol for a degree course at a reputable university, but this route is not open to everyone who would like to learn something about the subject. Furthermore, some prudent people may have the good sense to want to find out something about psychology *before* committing themselves to a long and perhaps expensive venture into higher education.

There are several other possibilities. Adult education centres often provide short introductory courses in psychology through evening classes or summer schools. These courses are generally interesting and enjoyable, but they tend to be pitched at a rather superficial level and to cover a restricted range of popular topics. Another possibility is to consult some of the introductory psychology textbooks that are available in bookshops and public libraries. Unfortunately, surveys conducted by academic psychologists have shown that elementary texts tend to present a biased and misleading view of the subject. An intrepid way of trying to teach yourself psychology is by consulting the primary sources – the technical articles containing original research findings in journals that can be found in university libraries. But you would probably find this exercise strangely frustrating and unrewarding, because the technical articles presuppose a knowledge of basic concepts, research methods, and statistical techniques without which most of them are impenetrable.

If you have no previous acquaintance with psychology, then chapter 2 should help to give you a close-up view of some of the nuts and bolts of the subject. It contains concrete examples of psychological research from a wide and representative range of the topics covered in degree courses. I have made no attempt to disguise the fact that parts of psychology are difficult or to patronize my readers. I assume that anyone who has chosen to read this book is serious about wanting to know what the subject is really like. But everything is explained in simple language and no previous knowledge is assumed. The examples are presented in the form of a self-assessment quiz. After completing the quiz and studying the answers and explanations carefully, you will certainly know something about psychology.

Further reading

The problem of defining psychology is a sterile one and is probably not worth pursuing any further. The concept of the category mistake was first proposed by Gilbert Ryle in his influential though controversial book *The concept of mind* (London: Hutchinson, 1949), and a more general review of approaches to the mind–body problem is provided by John Heil in *The philosophy of mind: A contemporary introduction* (London: Routledge, 1998). An interesting discussion of the mind–body problem in relation to the problem of consciousness is contained in Daniel C. Dennett's *Consciousness explained* (London: Penguin, 1991).

An excellent brief overview of psychoanalysis by Peter Fonagy, who is a professor of psychoanalysis and also a practising psychoanalyst, is contained in *Applications of psychology*, edited by me, Andrew M. Colman (London & New York: Longman, 1995, chapter 5), and a more detailed review of psychoanalysis, with many clinical illustrations, is provided by Fred Pine in *Diversity and direction in psychoanalytic technique* (New Haven, CT: Yale University Press, 1998). Robyn M. Dawes's *House of cards: Psychology and psychotherapy built on myth* (New York: Free Press, 1994) contains a penetrating and intriguing critique of psychoanalysis, psychiatry, and psychotherapy in general.

An excellent account of the uses and abuses of IQ testing is provided by Mark Snyderman and Stanley Rothman in *The IQ controversy, the media and public policy* (New Brunswick, NJ: Transaction, 1990), and a judicious survey of IQ and mental testing is provided by Nicholas J. Mackintosh in *IQ and human intelligence* (Oxford: Oxford University Press, 1998). Jean Piaget's experiment on children's perception of morality, using the story of the broken cups, is reported in chapter 2 of his book *The moral judgment of the child* (London: Routledge & Kegan Paul, 1932).

The best short introduction to moral philosophy or ethics is John Mackie's *Ethics: Inventing right and wrong* (Harmondsworth: Penguin, 1977), and a fuller survey is provided by Harry J. Gensler in *Ethics: A contemporary introduction* (London: Routledge, 1998). John Beloff's *Parapsychology: A concise history* (New York: St Martin's, 1994) provides a balanced historical survey of parapsychology. Peter L. Berger's *Invitation to sociology: A humanistic perspective* (New York: Anchor, 1963) is still one of the best short introductions to sociology, and Ken Morrison's *Marx, Durkheim, Weber: Foundations of modern social thought* (London: Sage, 1995) focuses more specifically and at a more advanced level on the three most influential social theorists.

Chapter 2

Beyond common sense

A self-assessment quiz

This chapter aims to present you with a wide range of examples of the research that psychologists do. This is the best way, and perhaps the only way, of giving you a true insight into the nature and scope of the subject. Abstract discussions *about* psychology will make more sense to you after your appetite has first been whetted by an hors-d'œuvre of concrete examples. The examples are presented as a series of questions and answers, partly to highlight the fact that psychology is a problem-solving activity, and partly to make the chapter more fun to read. There may be a grain of truth in the belief that psychologists love giving people tests, and it is certainly true that people love taking tests, or at any rate some people do. Quiz addicts may therefore find this chapter entertaining and challenging as well as informative. But you will not be able to sail through it effortlessly. It is only fair to warn you that the quiz is hard.

Someone once asked George Bernard Shaw whether he could play the violin. "I don't know," Shaw replied, "I've never tried." If anyone ever cracked the same joke about understanding behaviour and mental experience rather than playing the violin, it would not raise many laughs. Why not? It takes just as long to become a psychologist as a violinist. Perhaps the reason is that most people think that they understand behaviour and mental experience rather well without the benefit of any formal training. The world is full of enthusiastic amateur psychologists who have never opened a book on the subject. Everyone knows that it takes specialized knowledge and training to learn to play a musical instrument, but some people regard psychology as nothing more than common sense dressed up in fancy language. Psychology is different from other subjects in this respect. No one expects to understand the behaviour of molecules, atoms and quarks without studying physics, for example, but many people do expect to understand human behaviour and mental experience without studying psychology. This is a fallacy, as the quiz will demonstrate rather brutally, at the cost of some embarrassment to those who think they know it all already. Without specialized knowledge or training you will find the questions very puzzling, because much of what psychologists have discovered is simply not available to intuition. Common sense is a poor guide in psychology as in any other branch of science. It expects research to confirm what everyone knows already, and it therefore assumes that nothing surprising or new can be discovered by research. If this were true, then there would be no need for psychology or any other research-based subject.

I urge you to try your hardest to answer the questions before reading my answers and explanations. Then even if you get all the answers wrong, your interest in the problems will have been aroused and you will be much more impressed by the right answers when you read them.

Instructions

Tackle the questions in any order. Record your answers on a sheet of paper together with the few words that you will sometimes have to write to earn bonus points. Note that for some of the questions more than one of the answers is correct and you will score no points if you choose only one of them, and for others all of the answers are wrong and you will score no points if you choose any of them. Answers and detailed explanations, with references in case you want to pursue the topics in greater depth, follow the questions. An interpretation of scores is given at the end of the chapter. Good luck!

Questions

1   How long do dreams last? In *A Midsummer Night's Dream* (I.i) Lysander describes true love as "brief" and "momentary" like a dream, which of course implies that dreams are brief and momentary. "The course of true love never did run smooth", Lysander adds, it is "Swift as a shadow, short as any dream". Do dreams really come and go in an instant as Shakespeare apparently believed? Do you think a typical dream lasts: (a) a

fraction of a second; (b) a few seconds; (c) a minute or two; (d) many minutes; (e) a few hours? Take a second point for correctly answering the following question about yourself. How often do you dream? (f) hardly ever or never; (g) about once every few nights; (h) about once a night; (i) several times every night.

2   Michael was exhausted from overwork. He slumped into bed and fell into a deep sleep almost immediately. After a while he began to twist and turn and call out "Please don't, please don't" over and over again. His wife, who was lying beside him, was understandably disturbed by this. She wondered whether she ought to wake him up in case he was having a nightmare or was about to start sleep-walking. When do sleep-walking and sleep-talking occur? (a) usually during nightmares; (b) usually during ordinary dreams; (c) neither.

3   This is a straightforward question (or is it?) about the wiring of the human visual system. Attached to the retina at the back of each eye are nerves that transmit visual information to the brain. Are the nerve fibres from the left eye connected to: (a) the left half of the brain; (b) the right half of the brain; (c) the pineal gland in the centre of the brain? Take a bonus point if you can describe more or less correctly the pathways to the brain of fibres from the touch-sensitive nerve endings in the skin and from the nerve cells that respond to sound vibrations in the ears.

4   John's childish curiosity led him to the kitchen where his mother was baking a cake for his ninth birthday. On the kitchen table were two identical bottles of milk. He watched his mother open one of the bottles and pour the milk into a wide glass  bowl. His eyes roved from the bowl to the bottle that was still full of milk and back to the bowl. His mother suddenly remembered something that she had read in *What is Psychology?* and decided to do a little experiment. "Tell me, clever boy,"

she said, "is there more milk in the bottle or the bowl?" Is John likely to have thought that: (a) the bottle contained more milk; (b) the bowl contained more milk; (c) the bottle and the bowl contained the same amount of milk?

5　Chapter 9 of the Gospel according to St John is devoted entirely to an episode in which Jesus restored the sight of a man "which was blind from his birth", and a briefer account of the same incident is given in Mark (8: 22–26). It appears that Jesus spat on the blind man's eyes, touched them with his hands, and then asked him whether he could see. "And he looked up, and said, I see men as trees, walking." Jesus was evidently not entirely satisfied, because he touched the man's eyes once again. This seems to have done the trick: "He was restored, and saw every man clearly."

More recently, surgical rather than miraculous methods have occasionally been used to restore the sight, late in life, of people born blind. During the first few days after the bandages are removed, do such people: (a) see nothing at all; (b) see only a blur; (c) see only vague shapes moving about, like the blind man in the Bible following Jesus' first attempt; (d) recognize familiar objects without touching them; (e) recognize objects by sight only after touching and looking at them simultaneously; (f) see everything upside-down?

6　This question has a sting in its tail. Hans, the butler, noticed that one of the light bulbs in the master bedroom of the east wing needed replacing. He climbed up a stepladder until the light bulb was at eye level. His head and shoulders were completely surrounded by a large drum-shaped parchment lampshade that hung from the light fitting. As he tried to unscrew the faulty bulb, the lampshade began to rotate around him to the right. At that moment Hans froze. He was suddenly aware of a mysterious buzzing noise. A large bee was hovering outside the rotating lampshade a short distance in front of his nose. From which

direction do you suppose Hans thought the sound was coming? (a) from in front; (b) from behind; (c) from the left; (d) from the right; (e) from above; (f) from below. Take a bonus point if you can give the correct reason for the answer.

7   You may be flattered to learn, especially if you think you are tone deaf, that under ideal listening conditions you can probably just hear the difference in pitch between a musical tone of 1000 hertz (cycles per second) and one of 1003 hertz. If the first tone were 2000 hertz, that is, exactly an octave higher than before, which of the following tones would you be able to distinguish from it? (a) 2001 hertz; (b) 2002 hertz; (c) 2003 hertz; (d) 2004 hertz; (e) 2005 hertz.

Take a second point for correctly answering the following question. Under ideal viewing conditions, which of the following light intensities would seem noticeably brighter than one from a light bulb of 1000 watts? (f) 1001 watts; (g) 1002 watts; (h) 1003 watts; (i) 1006 watts; (j) 1012 watts; (k) 1018 watts; (l) 1024 watts.

8   Gustav was trying to read *What is Psychology?* by the light of a single candle in order to save electricity – he was an eccentric old man. His eyes began to ache, and he grudgingly admitted to himself that the level of illumination needed to be doubled. How many further candles would have to be lit to make the illumination seem twice as bright? (a) 1; (b) 2; (c) 3; (d) 4; (e) 5; (f) 6; (g) 7; (h) 8; (i) 9; (j) 10.

Now, for a second point, consider the following closely related problem. Smith was a creative but absent-minded chef. He prepared two sauces, A and B, according to the same recipe apart from the amount of salt used in each. "This one's delicious" said one of the dinner guests, pointing to Sauce B. "Could you give me the recipe, Smith?" "Oh dear," replied Smith, "I can't for the life of me remember how much salt went into that one." The dinner guests tasted the two sauces, carefully comparing them for saltiness. The consensus of opinion was that Sauce B tasted twice as salty as Sauce A. "Ah, well," beamed Smith, "I remember putting a quarter of a teaspoon of salt into Sauce A, so there must be half a teaspoon in Sauce B." One of the dinner guests who had once read *What is Psychology?* thought for a moment and then announced that

Sauce B contained: (k) less than half a teaspoon of salt; (l) more than half a teaspoon of salt; (m) half a teaspoon of salt, give or take a few grains. Take a well-deserved bonus point for correctly stating the general law that underlies both problems.

9   Frank's wife invented the following game while the couple were relaxing on a beach on holiday. Frank closed his eyes while his wife tapped his forearm gently with a pencil, and he tried to guess the exact spots where she had tapped. On each occasion, she followed a fixed procedure. She gave a warning tap, paused for a second, then tapped the same spot and another spot several centimetres away in quick succession, with a gap of about one tenth of a second. Frank then opened his eyes and pointed to the spots where he thought he had been touched. Where do you suppose that Frank felt the taps? (a) the first and second taps close to their actual position and the third tap about half its actual distance away; (b) the first and second taps close to their actual positions and the third tap about twice its actual distance away; (c) the first and third taps close to their actual positions and the second tap about half-way between them; (d) the first tap close to its actual position, the second tap close to the actual position of the third tap, and the third tap about twice its actual distance from the other taps.

When she got bored with the game, Frank's wife transferred it to his chest, keeping to the same timing. She delivered the first (warning) tap and the second tap close to his breastbone, and the third tap a few centimetres away on the other side of his chest. For a bonus point, describe in words where Frank must have felt the three taps in this version of the game.

10 On a trip to the local supermarket with Fred, Georgina came across two brands of canned kidney beans. One of the cans was twice as wide and twice as deep as the other, but to Georgina's surprise they were similarly priced, and the labels showed that they both weighed 250 grams. "There's probably more water in the smaller one," she thought. She decided to play a little trick on Fred. She moved the self-adhesive price tags so as to cover the weights that were marked on the labels, and she then showed the cans to Fred. "Fred darling," she said, "I've got a problem. Are you any good at judging weights?" "I am rather,

and I can tell you've lost a bit of weight," replied Fred, playfully lifting Georgina off the ground. "I'm not sure which of these two cans of kidney beans is heavier," she lied. "What do you think? Take your time feeling them." After lifting the cans and holding them for a while, what did Fred probably reply? (a) the smaller can feels slightly heavier; (b) the smaller can feels much heavier; (c) the larger can feels slightly heavier; (d) the larger can feels much heavier; (e) neither can feels noticeably heavier than the other.

11 Edwin put a black-and-white film into a camera, fitted a green filter over the lens, and photographed a bowl of fruit. Without moving the camera, he took another picture of the fruit with a red filter over the lens. He made black-and-white transparencies of both pictures. He projected the first black-and-white transparency on to a screen from a slide projector, and the image consisted of various shades of grey. He then projected the second black-and-white transparency from a different slide projector, using a red filter over its lens, and of course this second image consisted of various shades of pink and red. Finally, he moved the two slide projectors as close together as possible and superimposed the two images onto the same screen. How do you suppose the composite image appeared? (a) entirely in shades of grey; (b) entirely in shades of pink and red; (c) partly in shades of grey and partly in shades of pink and red; (d) in full natural colour, with red strawberries, green apples, blue plums, yellow bananas, and so on.

12 "We'll have an ongoing strike situation on our hands unless we can get the workforce to understand that their pay demand will simply be too costly for the company to meet, and when I say costly, ladies and gentlemen, I'm talking telephone numbers," said the company chairman. "I think Leon should go outside and factualize the scenario to them." Leon lowered his eyes. "I don't fancy that idea much," he said. "I personally think the pay demand is reasonable." "My dear chap," said the chairman, "*you* don't have to believe what you tell them, at the end of the day it's the *workers* who have got to believe it. And the company would certainly appreciate your cooperation in this small matter. Need I say more?" With these words, the chairman reached into his desk and handed Leon some cash. Leon then

went out and succeeded in persuading the assembled workers that their pay demand was unreasonable. When he got home that evening, he fixed himself a strong drink, stretched out on a sofa, and mulled over the events of the day. Do you think that, by then, his personal attitude towards the workers' pay demand is likely to have become: (a) less favourable; (b) more favourable; (c) neither less favourable nor more favourable? For a second point, try to answer the following closely related question. Is Leon's attitude more likely to have changed: (d) if he was paid a small amount of money; (e) if he was paid a large amount of money?

13   Hermann advertised a course of memory training in his local newspaper. The training method was based on a pack of twenty cards, each of which had a nonsense syllable such as DAX or KEB typed on it. Everyone who enrolled for the course had first of all to memorize the twenty nonsense syllables in the following way. They went through the pack once, examining each card for a few seconds, and then they wrote down as many of the nonsense syllables as they could remember. They repeated this procedure over and over again until they recalled all twenty items correctly.

The next day, Hermann instructed his trainees once again to write down as many of the nonsense syllables as they could remember, without looking at the cards again. On this test, do you suppose that: (a) quick learners remembered more items that slow learners; (b) people with good memories remembered more items than people with poor memories; (c) most people remembered about the same number of items? Take a second point for correctly answering the following question. Suppose Hermann had used meaningful words, which are easier to learn than nonsense syllables. If all other aspects of the procedure were kept the same, then on the second day would the trainees on average have remembered: (d) more items; (e) fewer items; (f) about the same number of items?

14   This is a question about little furry animals. Burrhus put one of his pet rats into a box. To avoid the bother of feeding it, he fitted the box with a lever that delivered a food pellet whenever the rat pressed it. After pressing the lever 150 times to get its rewards, the rat had clearly acquired a habit, because it

continued to press the lever regularly although there were no food pellets left in the machine. Burrhus repeated the procedure with a second rat. By this time he was running short of food pellets, so he set his machine to deliver them irregularly, on average once every five lever-presses. After this rat had pressed the lever 150 times, it had also acquired a habit that persisted although the food pellets were no longer forthcoming.

Do you suppose that after this training: (a) the first rat displayed the habit for longer than the second; (b) the second rat displayed the habit for longer than the first; (c) the rats displayed the habit for about the same length of time; (d) the first rat showed neurotic behaviour; (e) the second rat showed neurotic behaviour; (f) both rats showed neurotic behaviour?

15   The influential philosopher Friedrich Nietzsche suffered from insanity and general ill-health for the last twenty years of his life. On the other hand, the great physicist Albert Einstein was perfectly sane and enjoyed good health throughout most of his three score years and sixteen. Are exceptionally intelligent people in general: (a) less physically and mentally healthy than others; (b) more physically and mentally healthy than others; (c) similar to others in physical and mental health; (d) less mentally healthy but similar to others in physical health; (e) less physically healthy but similar to others in mental health?

16   This question touches on the delicate issue of social class and the even more delicate issue of mental disorder. Do you suppose that schizophrenia, the most common of the serious mental disorders in industrial societies, is: (a) more common among unskilled working-class people than among the upper middle class; (b) more common among upper-middle-class people than among unskilled workers; (c) about equally common in all social classes? Take a bonus point for correctly answering the same question with respect to autistic disorder (or autism), a mental disorder of infancy and childhood that resembles schizophrenia in many ways.

17   Most people have heard of the psychological disorder of multiple or split personality represented in Robert Louis Stevenson's *The Strange Case of Dr Jekyll and Mr Hyde*, in

which an individual alternates between two or more distinct personalities. Is this disorder classified as: (a) manic–depressive psychosis; (b) schizophrenia; (c) neither?

18 A group of friends decided to put some money into a kitty and spend it at the race track on Derby day. Before each race they wrote down their private opinions about the bet that ought to be placed. The most cautious decision was not to place a bet at all, a more risky decision was to place a small bet on a horse with favourable odds of winning, and a very risky decision was to place a large bet on an outsider. After considering their individual opinions, the group members assembled to discuss their individual opinions and to arrive at a joint decision. Compared to the average of the individual decisions, are the group decisions likely to have been: (a) more cautious; (b) more risky; (c) neither more cautious nor more risky?

19 This question is designed to test your knowledge of sex. Which of the following do you suppose are common to all known human societies? (a) prohibition of sex between certain close relatives; (b) knowledge of the connection between sexual intercourse and pregnancy; (c) general disapproval of homosexuality.

20 Bibb was sitting in a dentist's waiting-room preparing himself mentally for the minor ordeal of a check-up. There was no one else in the room. He suddenly noticed smoke billowing through a vent in the wall. The smoke quickly filled the room, obscuring Bibb's vision and interfering with his breathing. With a mounting sense of danger, he rose to his feet and tried unsuccessfully to peer through the vent. Eventually, 2 minutes after first noticing the smoke, he dashed out of the waiting-room and alerted the dentist's receptionist. His prompt action enabled the fire to be extinguished in the nick of time.
    Suppose that there had been two other patients in the waiting-room with Bibb when the smoke appeared. Do you think that: (a) Bibb would probably have reported the fire sooner; (b) at least one of the three would probably have reported the fire sooner; (c) Bibb would probably have reported the fire after about the same lapse of time; (d) at least one of the three would probably have reported the fire after about the

same lapse of time; (e) Bibb and the others would probably have failed to report the fire in time?

Answers and explanations

1 (d, i)   Score one point for realizing that a typical dream lasts many minutes (generally about 20 minutes) and a second point for knowing that you dream several times every night (everyone does). You may think that you dream much less than this, because you probably remember only fragments of dreams that occur just before you wake up.

These research findings arose from the accidental discovery in 1952 of a reliable behavioural indicator of dreaming. Eugene Aserinsky, a graduate student at the University of Chicago, noticed rapid eye movements occurring behind the closed eyelids of sleeping infants. By waking adult sleepers during or immediately after an episode of rapid eye movement (REM), William Dement and Nathaniel Kleitman were able to show that REM sleep is associated with vivid and intense dreaming. It is now known that some mental activity, more akin to vague thinking than dreaming, occasionally occurs during non-REM sleep, but full-blown dreams occur only in REM sleep.

Information about the electrical activity of the brain during sleep has come from electroencephalogram (EEG or brain-wave) studies. The EEG provides a continuous record of voltage changes via electrodes fixed to the scalp. Although it is more difficult to awaken someone from REM sleep than from dreamless non-REM (or slow-wave) sleep, the EEG patterns associated with REM sleep resemble those of wakefulness rather than non-REM sleep, and for this reason REM sleep is sometimes called paradoxical sleep.

Many thousands of people, including some who have claimed that they never dream, have been investigated in sleep laboratories since the early 1950s, and virtually all of them have shown several dreaming episodes every night spent sleeping. The only case on record of a person who did not dream at all and showed no REM activity during sleep was a man with shrapnel head wounds discovered by the Sleep Research Centre in Haifa, Israel, in 1984. Ordinary adults spend about 20 per cent of their sleeping time dreaming. Infants and young children spend even more – about 50 per cent. Adults enter REM sleep roughly every 90 minutes while asleep, which means that they normally experience four or five dreaming episodes every night. The episodes grow longer towards morning, the first typically occupying only 5 or 10 minutes and the last half an hour or more. Contrary to popular superstition dating back at least to Shakespeare's time, dreams are generally in real time in the sense that they last roughly as long as the events that are being dreamt about.

There is indirect evidence that REM sleep in general, or perhaps dreaming in particular, serves a biological function, although the function is not known. In a number of experiments, sleepers were deprived of REM sleep by being awakened whenever they showed rapid eye movements and were then allowed to go back to sleep again. For purposes of comparison, other sleepers were deprived of the same amount of dreamless non-REM or slow-wave sleep. When they were later allowed to sleep normally without interruption, the experimental group who had been deprived of REM sleep, but not the ones deprived of non-REM sleep, compensated by having more and longer REM episodes. The longest dream ever recorded occurred in a person who had been deprived of REM sleep in an experiment at the University of Illinois in 1967. It lasted 2 hours and 23 minutes.

References

Aserinsky, E., & Kleitman, N. (1953). Regularly occurring periods of eye motility and concomitant phenomena during sleep. *Science, 118,* 273–274.

Dement, W.C. (1978). *Some must watch while some must sleep.* New York: Norton.

Hobson, J.A. (1995). Sleep and dreaming. In D. Kimble, & A.M. Colman (Eds), *Biological aspects of behaviour,* (pp. 68–91), London & New York: Longman.

* * *

2 (c)   Score one point for knowing that sleep-walking and sleep-talking (with clearly enunciated words) do not occur during nightmares or ordinary dreams, although film makers and novelists often assume that they do. There is a rather interesting reason why they do not occur in nightmares and dreams.

Sleep is often regarded as a state of complete relaxation and inactivity. But during rapid eye movement or REM sleep (see the answer to Question 1), when the sleeper's mind is filled with vivid and intense dreams, the electrical activity of the brain resembles wakefulness more closely than it does dreamless sleep. For example, a sleeper in this state may dream about talking to a friend, playing tennis, or chasing a bus, but these ideas are not translated into the bodily actions that would accompany them in the waking state. In fact, during REM sleep the skeletal muscles of the sleeper's body – the voluntary muscles that control movements of the limbs and joints – are completely paralysed and atonic, lacking tone or tension. The only observable bodily movements in a person in REM sleep, apart from breathing and rapid eye movements, are occasional twitches of the extremities.

The brain mechanism responsible for sleep paralysis during REM episodes was discovered in 1965 by Michel Jouvet and F. Delormé of the University of Lyons in France. It is situated in the brainstem, the stalk-like structure at the bottom of the brain that links the brain to the spinal cord and contains structures that control consciousness and certain vegetative functions such as breathing and the operation of the heart and liver. Experiments on cats revealed that if a small volume of tissue in a part of the brainstem called the pons is destroyed with a heated wire, then the cats do not lie still during REM sleep. As soon as a REM episode begins they start to move about. They raise their heads, twitch their whiskers, stand up, make movements typical of stalking and attacking prey, hiss, spit, and paw the air, although they are fast asleep and their movements are not directed at anything in the environment. This is called REM sleep without atonia. The mechanism that causes atonia during REM episodes prevents people from acting out their dreams and possibly injuring themselves. It is thought by some researchers that the signals to the body from the brainstem are similarly switched off in the disorder called narcolepsy, in which sudden and unpredictable lapses occur from wakefulness directly into REM sleep or from wakefulness into paralysis and atonia without loss of consciousness.

References

Chase, M.H., & Morales, F.R. (1990). The atonia and myoclonia of active (REM) sleep. *Annual Review of Psychology, 41*, 557–584.

Hobson, J.A. (1995). *Sleep*. San Francisco: W.H. Freeman.

Jouvet, M., & Delormé, F. (1965). Locus coeruleus et sommeil paradoxal. *Comptes-rendus de la Société Biologique, 159*, 895–899.

Morrison, A.R. (1983). A window on the sleeping brain. *Scientific American, 248(4)*, 86–94.

*   *   *

3   Score one point for realizing that none of the suggested answers is correct, and a bonus point for describing the pathways to the brain for touch and hearing more or less correctly (see below).

The pathways for vision are complicated. The retina at the back of each eye is divided into two halves. The lens of the eye focuses light from the centre of the visual field – the point on which the gaze is fixated – onto the fovea in the middle of the retina. Light from the left half of the visual field falls on the right halves of both retinas, and light from the right visual field falls on the left halves of the retinas. The nerve fibres from *one half* of each retina cross to the opposite side of the brain, and the rest are uncrossed and are connected to the corresponding hemisphere of the brain. The crossed fibres are the ones from the inner or nasal halves of the retinas – the halves nearest to the bridge of the nose – and the uncrossed fibres are those from the outer halves.

It is not too difficult to work out from the peculiar wiring diagram of the human visual system that all images from the left visual field are transmitted to the right hemisphere of the brain. These are images that fall on the inner or nasal half of the left retina and the outer half of the right retina. Conversely, images from the right visual field are transmitted by both eyes to the left hemisphere of the brain. In other (and fewer) words, images from each half of the visual field (not each eye) are sent to the opposite hemisphere of the brain.

Certain types of blindness following head injury baffled psychologists and medical specialists before the pathways were properly understood. The area of the brain to which optical signals are eventually sent is the visual cortex. It consists of areas of the two hemispheres at the very back of the brain. People whose right visual cortex is badly damaged, usually by injury or a massive stroke, lose vision in both eyes for the left visual field, and people with left visual cortex damage are blind in the right visual field. Astonishingly, people with these forms of semi-blindness are often unaware of the fact that half the visual field has disappeared. Although they cannot see anything to one side of the point on which their gaze is fixed, they often go for months or years without noticing that anything is missing. They tend to bump into furniture and fail to notice things that other people see, but they cannot easily pinpoint their disability. The missing half of the visual field is not a conspicuous black patch like a cloth draped over one half of a television screen. It is simply not visible, like anything behind the head or outside the visual field of a person with normal vision. But a person with left homonymous hemianopia (as it is called) who gazes fixedly at the dot in the printed sequence L.R will see the R but not the L, and a person with right homonymous hemianopia will see the L but not the R. To test for these forms of blindness, the person is asked to close one eye and fixate on a point directly ahead while an object is waved in the area to the left and right of the fixation point, and then the procedure is repeated with the other eye.

The *partial decussation* or partial crossing over of the visual pathways was discovered by Isaac Newton in 1704. What is the function of such a seemingly complicated arrangement? The answer is that it plays an important part in stereoscopic depth perception. Researchers have found that in most fishes and birds the nerve fibres from the eyes are completely crossed, but that as animals evolved with eyes more towards the front of the head than the side, the percentage of uncrossed fibres increased. In mammals, the percentage of uncrossed fibres is related to the amount of overlap between the visual fields of the two eyes. For example, the rabbit has eyes on the sides of its head and only a small overlap in visual fields, and it therefore has only a tiny area that can be seen with both eyes at once, and the percentage of uncrossed fibres is correspondingly small. In human beings there is almost complete overlap of visual fields and almost half the fibres are crossed. Overlapping visual fields provide an extremely accurate form of depth perception called stereopsis. The distance of an object can be finely judged by the degree to which the images on the retinas differ from each other. Each eye records the visual field from a slightly different angle, so the retinal images are not quite identical, and the closer an object is to the eyes, the greater the disparity. This explains the importance of overlapping visual fields for depth perception. In order to compare the two images with each other, the brain must bring the nerve signals from both eyes together. The seventeenth-century French philosopher René Descartes thought that information from both eyes converged on the pineal gland in the centre of the brain (see chapter 5). It was later discovered that the pineal gland plays no such role, but the German physiologist Hermann von Helmholtz pointed out that there must nevertheless be *some* place where information from the two eyes is compared. He called this unknown place the Cyclopean eye, after the Cyclops in Greek mythology, which had an eye in the middle of its forehead.

In 1959 David Hubel and Torsten Wiesel of Harvard University discovered cells in the visual cortex that respond to information from both eyes and that came to be called binocular cells. Approximately half the neurons in the primary visual cortex at the back of the head are binocular cells, and some of them are disparity-selective in the sense that they respond only when the disparity between the two signals is within certain preset limits, thus providing a basis for stereoscopic depth perception. These are the Cyclopean eyes, and it is they that enable people and some other animals to locate objects in space by the method of comparing the images in the region where the visual fields overlap. This method of stereopsis is not available to animals whose visual fields do not overlap, and that is why their visual pathways are less complicated, with information from each eye going to the opposite side of the brain, but there are several other cues that provide information about visual depth.

The auditory pathways are also partly crossed, which is helpful for sound localization (see Question 6), but the crossed connections are much stronger than the uncrossed ones. Take your bonus point if you said that they are completely crossed, although that is not strictly true, or if you said that they are partly crossed, provided that you also gave the right answer about touch. The nerve pathways for touch (and movement) are completely crossed. No obvious function would be served by partial decussation in this case.

References

Pettigrew, J.D. (1972). The neurophysiology of binocular vision. *Scientific American, 227(2)*, 84–95.

Schiffman, H.R. (1996). *Sensation and perception: An integrated approach* (4th ed.). New York: Wiley.

Springer, S.P., & Deutsch, G. (1998). *Left brain, right brain: Perspectives from cognitive neuroscience* (5th ed.). New York: W.H. Freeman.

* * *

4 (c) Score one point. John is likely to have thought that the bottle and the bowl contained the same amount of milk. This was a trick question, because a child a few years younger would probably have thought that the bottle contained more milk than the bowl, and readers with a superficial knowledge of psychology may have fallen into the trap. The child in the question was 9 years old, and the great majority of children have mastered the conservation of substance, as it is called, by that age. The famous experiment on which the question was based and the underlying idea of conservation come from the work of the Swiss psychologist Jean Piaget (1896–1980).

The relevant part of Piaget's theory of intellectual development is the concept he called centration. Roughly speaking, this is a tendency among young children to focus attention on only one aspect of a problem at a time. One consequence of this is an inability to solve problems involving conservation. Conservation of number is illustrated by the following experiment that anyone with a young child can easily perform at home. Set up a row of eight egg-cups, each containing an egg, and ask the child to confirm that the number of egg-cups is the same as the number of eggs. Then tell the child to watch while you remove the eggs from the egg-cups one by one and place them close together in a row that is much shorter than the row of egg-cups. Then ask the child whether there are now more eggs than egg-cups, more egg-cups than eggs, or the same number of egg-cups and eggs. The experiment can of course be done with flowers and flower pots, cups and teaspoons, or any other suitably paired objects.

Most children under about 6½ or 7 years of age reply that there are more egg-cups than eggs, and the reason for this is that the row of egg-cups is longer than the row of eggs. The child focuses on the relative *lengths* of the rows without taking into account their relative *densities* or the fact that nothing has been added or taken away. This is an example of what Piaget called centration, and in this example it leads to a failure to conserve number. Interestingly, even a child who has learnt to count may make the same mistake. Children who can count but are too young to have attained the conservation of number sometimes count the eggs and the egg-cups correctly but still say that there are more egg-cups than eggs. They can go through the motions of counting but cannot grasp the abstract meaning of number or of words like *more*.

The experiment described in the question relates to conservation of substance. A young child centres on the greater height of the milk in the bottle than in the bowl, without taking into account the narrowness of the bottle compared with the bowl and the fact that the quantity of milk has not changed, and concludes that there must be more milk in the bottle. Tests for conservation of mass and volume traditionally make use of identical lumps of plasticine or play dough that can be moulded into different shapes and then weighed in a balance or immersed in water in front of the child.

The development of conservation, whether of number, substance, mass, or volume, proceeds through three phases. The child first centres on only one feature of the comparison, for example the lengths of the rows or the heights of the liquid, and gives the wrong answer consistently. During the second phase the child vacillates. In the final phase the child exhibits a mastery of conservation with complete decentration and has no difficulty taking more than one factor into account at a time and in giving the right answer.

The same sequence of development has been found among Swiss, English, American, and Canadian children, and even among children from cultures in Asia, Africa, and Latin America. The various types of conservation have generally been found to appear in the same order: first number and substance, then mass, then volume.

The typical ages at which these abilities are mastered vary slightly from one culture to the next. In a large survey of 1714 children in the United Kingdom during the standardization of the British Ability Scales it was found that only about 20 per cent of the 4–5-year-old children gave right answers to questions involving the conservation of substance and number, whereas about 80 per cent of the 7–8-year-old children answered correctly. Children who are 9 years old, like the boy in the question, almost always gave the right answer.

References

Piaget, J. (1952). *The child's conception of number* (Trans. C. Gattegno & F.M. Hodgson). London: Routledge & Kegan Paul. (Original work published 1941)

Piaget, J., & Inhelder, B. (1969). *The psychology of the child* (Trans. H. Weaver). London: Routledge & Kegan Paul. (Original work published 1966)

Singer, D.G., & Revenson, T.A. (1998). *A Piaget primer: How a child thinks* (revised ed.). Madison, CT: International Universities Press.

* * *

5 (d)   Score one point. People whose blindness is cured late in life are able to recognize familiar objects by sight without touching them. This question has been debated since the seventeenth century, but it was not satisfactorily resolved until psychologists investigated it carefully in the 1960s and 1970s.

In 1690 the English philosopher John Locke (1632–1704) speculated at length in his *Essay Concerning Human Understanding* (Book 2, chapter 9, section 8) about how the world might look to someone who suddenly acquired the gift of sight late in life. He thought that this experiment of nature could provide a crucial test for his empiricist ideas (see chapter 5). He was convinced that such a person would be quite unable at first to recognize even familiar objects by sight alone. To explain his reasons for believing this, he quoted a letter from his friend, "the learned and worthy Mr Molineux", actually the Irish philosopher, astronomer, and politician William Molyneux (1656–1698), who thought that a person who had only just acquired vision would not at first be able to distinguish a globe (ball) from a cube by sight alone: "For, though he has obtained the experience of how a globe, how a cube affects his touch, yet he has not yet obtained the experience that what affects his touch so or so must affect his sight so or so." This problem is called Molyneux's question.

Congenital blindness is extremely rare, fortunately for humanity but unfortunately for psychologists interested in the role of experience in vision, and when it is curable, it is even rarer for it to go untreated for very long. Total blindness, which results from serious injury or disease in the retinas or optic nerves of both eyes, or massive brain damage, has never been cured. The types of congenital blindness that have been treated successfully are caused by cataracts of the lenses or opacity of the corneas. In these cases the retinas were functioning normally and the patients therefore had some residual vision and were all able, at least, to tell light from darkness, but some were effectively blind in so far as they could not perceive the outlines of objects.

In 1932 the German researcher Marius von Senden scoured the world's medical literature and compiled a list of sixty-six cases of blindness cured late in life. Records of what the patients said and did after their operations seemed to suggest that they could not at first recognize or name common objects by sight alone. To revert to Locke's example, they could see the difference between a ball and a cube but they did not know which was which until they were allowed to handle them. The available evidence suggested that they could not even judge by sight which of two objects was larger. But none of von Senden's cases, the most recent of which had been reported in 1904, had been carefully examined, and there are many reasons for believing that the reports were unreliable.

In 1963 the British psychologists Richard L. Gregory and Jean G. Wallace reported the first rigorous investigation of late recovery from blindness. The patient was a man, 52 years of age, who had been blind since he was less than a year old and whose sight had been restored. Gregory and Wallace's report on S.B., as they called him, overturned von Senden's earlier conclusions and established several surprising facts.

There is little doubt that S.B. could recognize familiar objects, including tables, chairs, and beds, not immediately, but certainly within a day or two of the removal of his bandages. There is no question but that he could recognize certain things by sight without touching them. He could tell the time from a large clock high up on the wall. He could see the difference between motor cars, buses, and trucks from a distance by looking at them through the window of his hospital ward. He was able to produce a recognizable drawing of a hammer, an object that he had used but had never seen. Most impressively of all, he could read the printed capital letters on the cover of a magazine. He was familiar with the shape of capital letters, because as a blind person he had been taught to recognize them by touch in order to read embossed name plates. But, in the terms of Locke's analysis of Molyneux's question, he had not had the opportunity to compare the look and feel of capital letters.

S.B. was occasionally surprised by what he saw. He was disappointed by the drabness of most colours, which he had expected to be much brighter, and he was irritated by flaking paint. He was startled by the shape of the crescent moon, which he had always imagined as having the shape of a slice of cake! Luckily, he found his wife "just as bonny as I thought she would be".

In 1971 Alberto Valvo reported evidence from a number of further cases in Rome, and more recently Oliver Sacks reported a new case in the United States. The evidence corroborated the findings of Gregory and Wallace in all important details. In particular, Valvo confirmed that the Italian patients could immediately recognize by sight printed capital letters whose shapes they had previously learned by touch alone. Molyneux's question is now more or less resolved, and the evidence shows quite clearly that Locke was wrong.

It is worth mentioning a surprising psychological finding on which the older and more recent evidence seem to agree. This is the tendency for people who acquire the gift of sight late in life to become depressed. The case of S.B. turned out tragically when he became so dejected after his operation that he apparently committed suicide three years later, and there are numerous similar cases in von Senden's book. One of von Senden's cases was that of Maria Theresia von Paradis, a gifted pianist for whom Mozart wrote one of his concertos, whose blindness was reportedly cured with "animal magnetism" (see chapter 5) by the Viennese physician Franz Anton Mesmer in 1777. Although Mesmer was a quack and the case is highly controversial, Maria Theresia's comments on her feelings after the cure are typical: "How comes it that I now find myself less happy than before? Everything that I see causes me a disagreeable emotion. Oh, I was much more at ease in my blindness." One of the reasons for this young woman's depression may have been the fact that her fame as a performing musician depended largely on her blindness. She may have felt that she lost more than she gained when her blindness was cured, and other people may have reacted similarly. Or perhaps it is difficult for a person who has been blind for many years to adapt to such an abrupt and radical change.

References

Gregory, R.L. (1998). *Eye and brain: The psychology of seeing* (5th ed.). Oxford: Oxford University Press. Chapter 8.

Gregory, R.L., & Wallace, J.G. (1963). Recovery from early blindness: A case study. *Quarterly Journal of Experimental Psychology, Monograph Supplement 2*. Cambridge: Heffner. Reprinted in R.L. Gregory, *Concepts and mechanisms of perception* (1974, pp. 65–129), London: Duckworth.

Morgan, M.J. (1977). *Molyneux's question: Vision, touch and the philosophy of perception*. Cambridge: Cambridge University Press.

Valvo, A. (1971). *Sight restoration and rehabilitation*. New York: American Foundation for the Blind.

* * *

6 (e) Score one point for knowing that the sound would seem to come from above, and take a bonus point for explaining this startling illusion. Before giving the correct explanation, I must first to say a few words about how we locate sounds in ordinary circumstances.

Why do we have two ears rather than one? Perhaps the most important reason is for accurate sound localization, which requires the use of both ears. When a sound wave reaches an object such as a person's head, it either bends round it or is reflected or absorbed. If the pitch of the sound is low and its wavelength therefore long compared to the diameter of the head, then the wave bends round the head, whereas if the pitch is high and the wavelength short compared to the diameter of the head, then the sound wave is reflected or absorbed. Consequently, the way a sound is located depends on its pitch or wavelength.

One important clue to the location of a low-pitched sound in the horizontal plane is the difference in the time of arrival of the sound in the two ears. For example, when the sound comes directly from the left, it begins and ends earlier in the left ear, and any sudden changes in pitch or intensity also arrive there earlier. These differences are known collectively as transient disparity. In addition to them, throughout the duration of the sound, the peaks of the wave reach the left ear fractionally sooner, and this difference is called ongoing time disparity or phase delay. Both kinds of disparity are greatest when the sound comes directly from the left or right, and least when it comes from in front or behind. The human brain interprets the disparities with astonishing accuracy for judging the position of a sound source in the horizontal plane. Experiments have shown that in an open area with no reflecting surfaces, or a simulation of these conditions using earphones, low-pitched sounds can be located to within 10 degrees, or a minimum of about 2 degrees under ideal conditions. It is not difficult to calculate, given the speed of sound and the distance between the left and right ears, that people can therefore detect time differences between the movements of their two eardrums of less than one ten-thousandth of a second.

Localization of high-pitched sounds also depends on the use of both ears, but in these cases differences in intensity rather than time are detected and interpreted. Because a high-pitched sound has a wavelength shorter than the diameter of the head, a sonic shadow is formed on the side furthest from the sound source and the signal is therefore slightly weaker there. The difference in intensity depends on the location of the sound source in the horizontal plane. Once again, the difference is greatest for sounds coming directly from the left or right and least for sounds coming from in front or behind. This clue to the location of the source is used for sounds above about 1000 hertz or cycles per second, that is, about two octaves above Middle C. It is less accurate than the methods based on time disparities except for very high-pitched sounds with frequencies above 8000 hertz when the pinna, the part of the ear that sticks out of the head, becomes effective as a focusing device. Animals with very small heads, such as rodents, cannot use time differences for locating sounds because these differences are too tiny to be detected accurately. But their ears are sensitive to very high-pitched sounds whose wavelengths are shorter than the diameter of their heads, and these small animals use the sonic shadows formed by their heads to locate sounds.

Although disparities in time and intensity give useful information about the location of sound sources in the horizontal plane, they are useless for locating sound in the vertical dimension. For example, a sound coming directly from above the head reaches both ears at the same time and with equal intensity, but this is also true of sounds coming directly from the front or back, and without moving our heads, we cannot distinguish between these possibilities. But if the disparity between the signals reaching the two ears stays the same when the head is turned to the left or right, then the sound must be coming either from above or from below.

In 1940 the United States psychologist Hans Wallach performed an experiment in which a continuous sound source was kept directly in front of the listeners' noses by means of a device attached to their heads, even when they turned their heads to the left or right. Because these head movements did not alter the time or intensity disparities between the signals reaching their ears, the listeners all thought that the sound was coming directly from above. Their brains had performed a remarkable feat of measurement, calculation, and logical deduction, and had come up with the wrong answer. The mistake is easy to understand. Normally, if turning the head to the left or right produces no time or intensity disparities, it is logical to conclude that the sound is coming directly from above or below. Because we are terrestrial or earth-bound creatures, experience has taught us that in such cases it is nearly always coming from above.

The barn owl, which is not earth-bound, relies on its ears to locate field mice and other prey in total darkness. It can locate sound sources to within one degree in both the horizontal and vertical dimensions, more accurately than human beings or any other species that has been tested. The key to its ability is the asymmetrical construction of its ears. The barn owl's left ear points downward, and its right ear points upward. As a result of this, its left ear is more sensitive to high-pitched sounds from below and its right ear to high-pitched sounds from above. This enables it to locate sounds in the vertical dimension much more accurately than human beings, and to swoop on its prey with deadly accuracy, capitalizing on its famous soundless flight.

Hans Wallach also devised the experiment with the rotating drum on which the question was based. In that experiment the listeners sat motionless inside a rotating drum that had vertical stripes on the inside and created a slight illusion of passive movement called vection. Most people have experienced vection while sitting in a stationary train when another train on an adjacent track begins to move, creating an illusory sensation of being moved in the opposite direction. In Wallach's experiment, the rotating drum induced a sensation of rotating in the opposite direction. The sound source was directly in front, and because the listener was really stationary, there were no disparities between the time of arrival or intensity of the sound in the two ears. As before, the ears collected this information with great sensitivity, and the brain put it all together, performed some high-powered calculations and deductions, and concluded that the sound must be coming from above. The illusion is very powerful, and it persists even if the individual is aware of the true situation.

References

Knudsen, E.I. (1981). The hearing of the barn owl. *Scientific American,* *245(6),* 83–91.

Konishi, M. (1993). Listening with two ears. *Scientific American, 268(4),* 34–41.

Wallach, H. (1940). The role of head movements and vestibular and visual cues in sound localization. *Journal of Experimental Psychology, 27,* 339–368.

—— (1976). *On perception.* New York: Quadrangle/New York Times Book Co. Chapter 6.

* * *

7 (k, l)   Score one point for realizing that none of the tones would be distinguishable from the first and another point for correctly identifying only the 1018-watt and 1024-watt light bulbs as noticeably brighter than the 1000-watt bulb. To answer the first question, you have to know Weber's law, and to answer the second you have not only to know Weber's law but also to remember the Weber fraction for visual brightness.

In 1846 the German physiologist Ernst Heinrich Weber discovered a fundamental law of sensation. The easiest way to explain it is with an example. By lifting objects manually, most people can just barely feel the difference in weight between an object of 530 grams and one of 540 grams. How heavy do you think an object would have to be to feel just barely heavier than one of 1060 grams? The answer is not 1070 but 1080 grams. What is important is not the absolute but the proportional difference. According to the same rule, the difference between a weight of 265 grams and one of 270 grams is just barely detectable. The general law is that the smallest increase in weight that can be detected is proportional to the original weight, so that the heavier the weights, the larger the difference has to be in order for it to be just barely detectable. This is equivalent to saying that the *difference threshold* (or the *just noticeable difference*) between two weights is a constant fraction of the lighter weight. Numerous experiments have shown that this fraction is in fact 1/53 for weights lifted by hand, as the examples that I have presented illustrate.

After establishing this law for weight discrimination, Weber went on to show that the same general principle applies to sensations of the pitch of musical tones, the loudness of tones, the brightness of lights, and other sensory experiences. The simplicity of the law is surprising, although most people are probably dimly aware from everyday experience that perceived differences depend on relative rather than absolute physical differences. For example, it is obvious that a journey of 5 miles seems much shorter than one of 10 miles, whereas a journey of 100 miles seems hardly any shorter than one of 105 miles.

Weber was not a mathematically minded person, and he explained his idea only in words and examples. Nowadays, psychologists always express it mathematically. Mathematical symbols provide a compact way of saying the same thing with greater clarity and generality. The mathematical form of Weber's law is:

$$(\Delta I)/I = k.$$

In this formula, ΔI stands for the difference threshold or just noticeable difference in stimulus intensity – the difference threshold in the weights of objects, the frequency or amplitude of sounds, the intensity of lights, and so on. It is sometimes called the *difference limen* (*limen* being the Latin word for threshold). The Greek letter delta (Δ) stands for *difference*, and the Roman letter I for *intensity*, although it is interpreted loosely to include perceptible stimulus dimensions such as pitch. In the first example that I gave, involving objects weighing 530 grams and 540 grams, the difference threshold (ΔI) is equal to 10 grams. I is the physical intensity of the less intense stimulus, that is, $I = 530$ grams. Finally k is a constant called the *Weber fraction*. The Weber fraction is constant for any given type of sensory discrimination but differs from one type to the next.

The Weber fraction for lifted weights is 1/53, as the example shows. For pitch discrimination, $k = 1/333$; for loudness discrimination, $k = 1/11$; for visual brightness discrimination, $k = 1/62$; and so on. The important point to understand is that in each case the difference threshold ΔI, expressed as a fraction of the intensity of the lesser stimulus I, is a constant k.

Weber's law is remarkably accurate over most of the usable range of intensity for nearly all types of sensation, but like Boyle's law and many other laws in physics it breaks down at the extremes. For visual discrimination of various kinds, the law holds across 99.9 per cent of the range of intensities that can be tested without damaging people's eyes. For loudness discrimination, the Weber fraction remains obediently constant across no less than 999,999-millionths of the usable range. The range of frequencies over which vibrations can be heard as sounds extends from about 16 hertz to about 20,000 hertz, although the upper limit goes down as we get older, and the Weber fraction is 1/333 for all pitches above 500 hertz and is slightly larger for lower pitches.

Getting down to business and applying Weber's law to the first question, note that the difference threshold at 1000 hertz is given as 3 hertz. It follows from the law that $3/1000 = k = 0.003$. This agrees, incidentally, with the Weber fraction of 1/333 for pitch discrimination that has been established by experiment. At 2000 hertz we therefore have $(\Delta I)/2000 = 0.003$, which yields by simple arithmetic $\Delta I = 6$. In other words, a person would not be able to distinguish a tone of 2000 hertz from one of less than 2006 hertz. All frequencies suggested in the question are below this value, so none would be distinguishable from the original.

It may surprise you that the answers can be stated in a general way for all listeners. The answers are indeed valid for everyone whose ears and auditory nerves are intact. What about the fact that some people obviously have a better sense of pitch than others, and what about people who are tone deaf? The answer is that virtually anyone can be trained to recognize differences in pitch corresponding to the Weber fraction of $k = 1/333$ under ideal listening conditions. Tone deafness, so called, does not arise from any inability to *hear* differences in pitch but from an inability to *recognize* or *interpret* what is heard, in other words a tone deaf listener does not know what to listen for. The handicap is analogous to dyslexia (word blindness) in which there is also a failure to recognize or interpret what is perceived, rather than a failure of perception itself – no one assumes that a dyslexic child cannot see the letters on the page or tell them apart.

Turning to the second question, the first interesting point to note is that visual brightness discrimination is much less sensitive than auditory pitch discrimination. In fact pitch discrimination is the most sensitive sensory ability of human beings, as shown by the fact that its Weber fraction is smaller than that for any other type of sensory discrimination.

Even competent psychologists would be stumped by the second question unless they happened to remember that the Weber fraction for visual brightness discrimination is 1/62. Bearing this figure in mind, and applying Weber's law to the information supplied in the question, we find that $(\Delta I)/1000 = 1/62$, and a little arithmetic simplifies this to $\Delta I = 16$. This, of course, is the difference threshold implied by the question. A light bulb of 1016 watts or more would seem noticeably brighter than one of 1000 watts. Of the wattages listed, only the last two are bright enough.

References

Gescheider, G.A. (1997). *Psychophysics: The fundamentals* (3rd ed.). Hillsdale, NJ: Lawrence Erlbaum Associates.
Laming, D. (1995). Psychophysics. In R.L. Gregory, & A.M. Colman (Eds), *Sensation and perception* (pp. 97–123), London & New York: Longman.

* * *

8 (g, k)   Score one point for realizing that seven further candles would have to be lit, a second point for concluding that Sauce B contained less than half a teaspoon of salt, and a third bonus point for correctly stating the power law, or half a point for correctly stating Fechner's logarithmic law, both of which I shall explain. The question was a real stinker, and even specialists in the psychology of sensation and perception are unlikely to have scored full marks on it unless they happened to have certain crucial figures from the experimental literature at their fingertips.

We are concerned here, as in Question 7, with the relationship between (psychological) sensations and the (physical) stimuli that give rise to them. This area of research is therefore called psychophysics, and it is the oldest branch of experimental psychology. The central problem of psychophysics can be stated quite simply. How is the magnitude of a sensation related to the intensity of the stimulus? The relation is not a simple one, as the following *Gedankenexperiment* (imaginary experiment) will show. Imagine walking into a completely dark room and switching on a single 100-watt light, and then switching on a second 100-watt light. The physical intensity of the illumination would be doubled when the second light was switched on, but the room would not look twice as brightly lit, in fact it would look only slightly brighter than when just one light was on. At least in this case, the strength of sensation is not related to stimulus intensity in any simple or obvious way.

The first person to understand this problem clearly was the German philosopher and mystic Gustav Theodor Fechner (1801–1887). Fechner is one of the most colourful characters in the history of psychology. Some of his earlier books were devoted to discussing the comparative anatomy of angels and proving that the

moon is made of iodine. On the morning of 22 October 1850, before rising from his bed, a slightly more useful idea sprang into his mind like a revelation. It was that equal increases in sensation correspond to equal *proportional* increases in stimulus intensity, or to put it another way, the magnitude of a sensation increases by equal amounts as the physical intensity of the stimulus increases by equal proportions. For example, according to this rule the increase in apparent brightness caused by raising the physical power from 100 watts to 200 watts is the same as the increase caused by raising it from 200 to 400 watts. Alternatively, raising the physical illumination from 60 watts to 180 watts produces the same increase in apparent brightness as raising it from 100 to 300 watts. This is because the physical intensity of the stimulus (governed by the number of watts) increases by the same proportion in each case: in the first pair of examples it is doubled each time, and in the second it is trebled each time. Perhaps the simplest way to express Fechner's idea is to say that the magnitude of a sensation increases by equal steps as the stimulus increases by equal proportions.

Fechner thought he had discovered a solution to one of the

central problems of philosophy, namely the mind–body problem (see chapter 5). He spent the following ten years performing experiments to test the validity of his law for various types of sensation. For example, from 1855 to 1859 he made no fewer than 67,072 weight comparisons, using himself as both experimenter and experimental subject. In 1860 his *Elements of Psychophysics* was published. In this work he described psychophysics as "an exact science of the functional relation or relation of dependency between body and mind".

How can Fechner's law be expressed mathematically? Anyone who is familiar with logarithms knows that the common logarithms 1, 2, 3, 4, ... correspond to the numbers 10, 100, 1000, 10,000, ... The logarithms go up in equal steps as the numbers go up by equal proportions, or more precisely the logarithms increase by one unit for every tenfold increase in the numbers. Fechner therefore suggested that "the increase of sensation and stimulus stand in a similar relation to that of the increase of a logarithm and a number". If we represent the magnitude of sensation by ψ (the Greek letter psi, short for *psy*chological) and the stimulus intensity by ϕ (Greek phi, short for *phy*sical), Fechner's law can be expressed like this:

$$\psi = k \log \phi.$$

In this formula, k is simply a constant scale factor that varies from one kind of sensation to another.

For almost a century psychologists believed that Fechner's logarithmic law was basically valid, although its predictions did not always turn out to be quite accurate in experiments. Various practical uses were found for it. Probably the best known is the decibel scale of loudness. A decibel (dB) is one-tenth of a bel, the unit of loudness named after Alexander Graham Bell, the inventor of the telephone. Using Fechner's formula, with $k = 10$ and ϕ representing physical sound intensity, ψ gives the decibel level. On the decibel scale, conversational speech registers about 60 dB. If two people speak at once, the physical intensity of the sound is doubled, but the decibel level rises to only 63 dB, if four people speak at once, it goes up to 66 dB, and so on. The decibel scale is used by broadcasting and telephone engineers, and laws governing industrial and environmental noise are based on it all over the world.

Unfortunately, Fechner's law is not quite right. In two influential articles in 1953 and 1957, the Harvard University psychologist S. Smith Stevens suggested a slightly different law that yields much more accurate predictions. The power law, as it is called, makes predictions that are astonishingly exact when tested in the laboratory. According to Fechner's logarithmic law, equal increases in sensation correspond to equal proportional increases in stimulus intensity. According to the power law, equal proportional increases in sensation correspond to equal proportional increases in stimulus intensity, and the two proportions are not necessarily the same. For example, the sensation of loudness is doubled whenever the sound intensity is multiplied by 2.80. The mathematical expression of the power law is:

$$\psi = k\phi^n,$$

where ψ is the magnitude of the sensation, k is a constant scale factor that depends on the units of measurement, ϕ is the intensity of the stimulus, and n is an exponent or power, which is constant for a given type of sensation but varies from one type to the next.

The exponents for various types of sensation have been determined by experiment. For some types, such as visual brightness ($n = 0.33$), the exponents are smaller than 1. In these cases, when the stimulus intensity increases by a certain proportion, the magnitude of the sensation increases by a smaller proportion, as shown by the *Gedankenexperiment* of going into a dark room and switching on one light and then another. In these cases Fechner's logarithmic law and the power law give similar results. But when large exponents apply, as in the sensation of electric shock ($n = 3.5$) or tasting saltiness ($n = 1.4$), a given proportional increase in stimulus intensity produces an even greater proportional increase in sensation, and in these cases the power law gives much more accurate predictions. Fechner's law is an excellent approximation for some types of perception, but it is inferior to the power law for others.

Turning now to the first part of the question, note that the stimulus intensity is initially the light of a single candle, therefore $\phi = 1$. The exponent for visual brightness has been found in numerous experiments to be 0.33, therefore $n = 0.33$. When one candle is lit, the power law states that:

$$\psi = k(1)^{0.33}.$$

After a certain (unknown) number of further candles are lit, the sensation of brightness is doubled. In mathematical symbols,

$$2\psi = k(\phi)^{0.33}.$$

We must solve these equations simultaneously to find the value of ϕ. The easiest way of doing this is by dividing each side of the second equation by the corresponding side of the first, that is, dividing 2ψ by ψ and $k(\phi)^{0.33}$ by $\psi = k(1)^{0.33}$. This yields the equation $2 = \phi^{0.33}/1^{0.33}$, which simplifies to approximately $\phi = 8$. What this means is that an illumination eight times as intense as a single candle would cause the sensation of brightness to double. In other words, seven further candles would have to be lit.

In the second part of the question Sauce A contains a quarter of a teaspoon of salt and Sauce B contains an unknown amount ϕ. Sauce B tastes twice as salty as Sauce A. The dinner guest in the question presumably remembered that the exponent for tasting saltiness is greater than 1 and realized that Sauce B must therefore contain less than twice as much salt as Sauce A. But having come as far as this, it would be a pity not to give you the full solution. Putting all the known facts including the correct exponent of $n = 1.4$ into the two equations, one for each sauce, we get:

$$\psi = k(1/4)^{1.4},$$

$$2\psi = k(\phi)^{1.4}.$$

Once again, divide each side of the second equation by the corresponding side of the first,

$$2 = \phi^{1.4}/(1/4)^{1.4},$$

which can be solved to give $\phi = 0.4$. Sauce B therefore contained four-tenths or two-fifths of a teaspoon of salt. You get a bonus point for stating the power law, or half a point for stating Fechner's law. You do not get any extra points for working out the exact amount of salt in Sauce B, but you may award yourself ten gold stars.

References

Fechner, G.T. (1860). *Elemente der Psychophysik* (2 vols). Leipzig: Breitkopf & Härtel. (Vol. 1, Trans. H.E. Adler, 1966, *Elements of psychophysics*. New York: Holt, Rinehart & Winston)

Gregory, R.L. (1984). *Mind in science: A history of explanations in psychology and physics*. Harmondsworth: Penguin. Chapter 18, pp. 500–515.

Stevens, S.S. (1986). *Psychophysics: Introduction to its perceptual, neural, and social prospects*. New Brunswick, NJ: Transaction.

Yost, W.A., Popper, A.N., & Fay, R.R. (Eds). (1993). *Human psychophysics*. New York: Springer Verlag.

* * *

9 (c)   Score one point for supposing that Frank felt the first and third taps on his forearm close to their actual positions and the second tap about half-way between them, and take a bonus point for stating that he felt the first and third taps on his chest close to their actual positions and the second tap near the middle of his breastbone. These compelling illusions, which you can explore for yourself with two pencils and a fairly intimate friend, were first reported in 1972 by the Princeton University psychologist Frank Geldard.

In Geldard's basic experiment, three taps were delivered by a precision instrument to the forearm of each research participant or subject. The first (warning) tap preceded the others by a full second. The second tap, at the same spot as the first, and the third tap, 10 centimetres away, were delivered in quick succession, as described in the question. When the time interval between the second and third taps was less than a quarter of a second, something surprising happened: the subjects felt the second tap very distinctly at a point somewhere between the first and third taps. Because the second tap seems to leap from its actual position towards the position of the third tap, Geldard called the effect *sensory saltation* (from Latin *saltare*, to leap).

The extent of sensory saltation depends on how quickly the third tap follows the second. If the interval is more than a quarter of a second there is no saltation, and the second tap is felt close to its actual position. If the interval is reduced to a tenth of a second as in the question, the tap is felt about half-way towards the position of the third tap. If the interval is further reduced to a twentieth of a second, the second tap is felt three-quarters of the way towards the third tap, and with an interval of about a fiftieth of a second or less the second tap leaps all the way to the position of the third. Sensory saltation does not occur if the distance between the taps is too great. For example, on the forearm sensory saltation ceases if the distance is increased from 10 to 20 centimetres. The areas within which sensory saltation occurs vary in size and shape from one part of the body to another. The areas on the limbs are large and elongated, the area on the palm of the hand is smaller and round, and the area on the tip of the forefinger is very small and nearly round.

One important property of sensory saltation that you would have to have known or guessed to earn the bonus point arises from the fact that the touch-sensitive nerve endings in the skin on each side of the body are connected to the opposite hemisphere of the brain (see the answer to Question 3). One consequence of this left–right dichotomy is that sensory saltation never crosses the midline of the body. If the first and second taps are close to the middle of the chest and the third tap is a few centimetres away on the other side of the chest, then the second tap will leap only as far as the midline, even if the time interval between the second and third taps is very short. The same principle applies to the forehead, back, and abdomen: sensory saltation never crosses the midline. This suggests that the seat of the phenomenon is in the brain and not in the skin.

Overwhelming evidence for this has come from an ingenious experiment in which a small area of skin on the forearm was anaesthetized with procaine so that nothing could be felt in the affected area. The first and second taps were delivered on one side of the anaesthetized area and the third on the opposite side. If some mechanism in the skin were responsible for sensory saltation, then the second tap could not be felt in the anaesthetized area. But if sensory saltation is caused by a process occurring in the brain, then there is no reason why the second tap should not be felt in the deadened zone. The results of the experiment were quite clear: the second tap invariably leapt right into the anaesthetized area, proving beyond reasonable doubt that the phenomenon arises in the brain.

References

Geldard, F.A. (1975). *Sensory saltation: Metastability in the perceptual world*. Hillside, NJ: Lawrence Erlbaum Associates.

Geldard, F.A., & Sherrick, C.E. (1986). Space, time and touch. *Scientific American, 255(1)*, 85–89.

* * *

10 (b)   Score one point. Fred is almost certain to have thought that the smaller can felt much heavier than the larger one. The illusion is reliable and startlingly powerful. Experiments have shown that when two objects are of equal weight but one is markedly larger than the other, about 98 per cent of people judge the smaller object to be much heavier than the larger one and feel certain that they are right. You can easily construct your own apparatus for demonstrating the effect by putting pieces of lead or other heavy material in two containers of different sizes, surrounding the weights by sand to prevent them from moving about and from being visible if the containers are transparent. In an experiment in the United States, 100 military officers judged the smaller object (on average) to be between twice and three times the weight of the larger one, which was the same weight but twice the size in each dimension and hence eight times the volume. A pound of feathers does indeed *feel* much lighter than a pound of lead, and people who rely on subjective judgements of weight when they go shopping are likely to make big mistakes.

The phenomenon is called the size–weight illusion, or Charpentier's illusion, although it was discovered by the German psychologists Georg Elias Müller and Friedrich Schumann in 1889. It is not as easy to explain as it at first appears. The most obvious explanation, originally proposed by Müller and Schumann, revolves around the muscular effort exerted in lifting the weights. If the larger object is lifted after the smaller one, then more than sufficient muscular effort will be applied in the expectation that it is heavier, making it seem to fly into the air, and this may create the impression that it is lighter. If the smaller object is lifted after the larger one, then the whole explanation applies in reverse. Unfortunately, this theory came to grief in 1931 when an ingenious experiment showed that the illusion persists if the subjects' hands are resting palm-up on a table-top and the objects are placed on them by the experimenter. In these circumstances, of course, no muscular effort on the part of the subjects is involved.

The explanation suggested by the French psychologist Pierre Marie Augustin Charpentier in 1891 focused on the specific pressure, that is, the pressure per square centimetre, that the objects exert on the surface of the body. The smaller object, although it is no heavier than the larger one, obviously exerts more pressure per square centimetre on the hands, because the same mass is concentrated in a smaller region of contact with the skin. This applies whether the objects are lifted or placed on upturned palms resting on a table top. According to Charpentier, people judge the smaller object to be heavier because it exerts more specific pressure. This plausible theory did not last long. In 1894 Théodore Flournoy showed experimentally that the illusion was experienced even when the objects were lifted by threads held between thumb and forefinger. The areas of contact between the threads and the surfaces of the subjects' bodies were of course roughly equal, but the illusion remained and Charpentier's theory collapsed.

The British psychologist Robert Thouless suggested in 1931 that the illusion results from people's inability to judge weight without being influenced by density. If two objects weigh the same but differ in size, then by definition the smaller object is denser. According to Thouless, the apparent weight of an object is a compromise between its actual weight and its density; if two objects are equal in weight, the smaller object feels heavier because it is denser. This seems a reasonable suggestion as far as it goes, and several experiments carried out by the Chinese psychologist I. Huang tended to confirm it, but it does not actually explain anything. It is more like a restatement of the problem than an explanation.

The most popular explanation in recent years has been the expectancy theory championed since 1970 by the United States psychologist Norman Anderson. It is based on the assumption that there is a sense of surprise when the second object is lifted. A person who first lifts the larger object expects the second object to be lighter because it is smaller, and vice versa. According to this theory, the smaller object feels heavier than it actually is because it is heavier than it is expected to be in comparison with the larger object. The expectancy theory seems persuasive on the face of it, but it does not really fit all the known facts about the illusion. It rests on the assumption that a person has a false expectation on lifting the second object. But experiments have shown that the illusion persists even if the two objects are lifted over and over again, or if people are allowed to examine them thoroughly and weigh them in a balance. In these experiments the participants or subjects know what to expect when they lift the second object, and they are not surprised. But not only does the illusion fail to disappear or even to subside, as the expectancy theory would surely predict, but if anything it grows stronger.

Alert readers may have noticed a certain family resemblance between the size–weight illusion and the failure of young children to master the conservation of mass (see the answer to Question 4). A young child thinks that the mass of a lump of plasticine changes when it is moulded into a different shape. The size–weight illusion can be thought of as a different kind of conservation failure, adults behaving as though they think that the mass of an object changes if it is a different *size*. In other words, adults are apparently unable to master the conservation of mass when volume rather than shape is altered. An adult centres, as it were, on the difference in size between the two objects without taking sufficient account of difference in density. This is a kind of conservation failure that Piaget never mentioned. But the size–weight illusion is not due to any intellectual confusion between mass and density. I can testify from personal observation that even professors of physics experience it as vividly as anyone else.

Very young children do *not* experience the size–weight illusion. The tendency to experience it usually begins to emerge during the fourth year and is well developed by 6 years of age. A failure to experience the illusion after 6 years of age used to be regarded by some psychologists as a sign of mental handicap, called De Moor's sign.

Finally, it is worth mentioning an almost unbelievable version of the size–weight illusion that can be demonstrated with two blocks of identical length and breadth but markedly different depths. If the smaller object is about nine times as heavy as the larger one, then when the two blocks are fitted together snugly they feel lighter than the heavier object alone!

References

Crutchfield, R.S., Woodworth, D.G., & Albrecht, R.E. (1955). *Perceptual performance and the effective person*. San Antonio, TX: Air Force Personnel and Training Research Center.

Huang, I. (1945). The size-weight illusion in relation to the perceptual constancies. *Journal of General Psychology, 33*, 43–63.

Jones, L.A. (1986). Perception of force and weight: Theory and research. *Psychological Bulletin, 100*, 29–42.

——— (1988). Motor illusions: What do they reveal about proprioception? *Psychological Bulletin, 103*, 72–86.

* * *

11 (d)   Score one point for believing the incredible. The image does indeed appear in full natural colour. This astonishing fact about the way we see colours was discovered accidentally in 1959 by Edwin Land, the inventor of the Polaroid camera. It disproves the notion, which you may have been taught at school, that the colour of an object is determined simply and straightforwardly by the wavelength of the light that it reflects.

The fundamental properties of the rainbow were discovered by Isaac Newton in 1666. Later physicists examined the properties of light in greater detail and showed that the visible spectrum extends from wavelengths of about 425 nanometres (billionths of a metre, or millionths of a millimetre) at the violet end to about 740 nanometres at the red end. In the nineteenth century James Clerk Maxwell and Hermann von Helmholtz found that by mixing light from the red, green, and blue bands of the spectrum it is possible to produce any spectral colour and some other colours such as purple that are not found in the spectrum. They went on to propose a theory of colour vision based on these three primary colours. The unproved assumption behind this classical trichromatic (three-colour) theory was that the eye contains three separate mechanisms for responding to light, namely red receptors for responding to long waves, green receptors for medium waves, and blue receptors for short waves. According to this theory, any colour sensation is determined by the relative amount of stimulation of the three types of receptors. It was widely believed from that time onwards that the colour seen at any point in the field of vision could be fully explained by the wavelength or wavelengths of the light coming from it.

Land's experiment shows that this common belief is quite wrong. The light reflected by the screen is composed entirely of "red" and "white" light. According to classical notions, the mixture of red and white can produce nothing but shades of pink. If we remove the black-and-white slides from the two projectors, then the screen does indeed look pink, but the instant we slot them back into position the image leaps into colour: apples look green, plums look blue, and bananas look yellow. Even non-spectral colours such as browns and purples are clearly visible. Yet the slides are capable only of letting through more or less red and white light at any point.

Colour vision is more subtle and complicated than is commonly realized. There is no such thing, properly speaking, as "red", "white", or "green" light. The colours that we see are determined not by the absolute wavelengths of the light, but by the relative balance of long, medium, and short wavelengths across the visual field. The simple trichromatic theory grossly oversimplifies the process, but it contains a portion of the truth. In 1959, physiological research confirmed that the retina contains three types of cones, each maximally responsive to a different wavelength, but what is crucial is that all three cone types respond to a lesser degree to wavelengths extending across most of the visible spectrum. For example, the "red" cones respond maximally to long wavelengths, but they also respond, though more weakly, to medium-wave and even short-wave light. There are other cells in the retina whose rate of firing is speeded up by signals from one type of cone and slowed down by signals from the others. Only after this process of addition and subtraction has been completed is the information passed to the visual cortex.

Land's experiment is closely related to the apparent constancy of objects in natural light. If you read this book out of doors, then the wavelength of the light reflected by the paper changes from short in mid-afternoon daylight, to medium in leafy outdoor surroundings, to long just before a reddish sunset, but the paper always looks white. In fact, the objects we see usually remain constant in colour as the wavelength of the illumination varies. The reason for this is that the perceived colour of an object is not determined simply by the wavelength of the light that it reflects. The eye-brain computer measures the relative balance of short, medium, and long wavelengths *in relation to the rest of the visual field* by comparing the responses of the three types of cones. Light of a particular wavelength has no inherent colour in itself but may be perceived as virtually any colour depending on the range of wavelengths in the surrounding visual field.

Land's experiment simply mimics something that occurs naturally. In certain circumstances the ambient outdoor illumination at sunset can result in everything reflecting various shades of "pink" light. All three primary colour receptors in the eye respond to differing degrees to the light reflected by a particular object, and the brain deduces the colour of the object by computing the relative responses of the three cone receptors and discounting the overall bias towards pink in the visual field. Everything appears naturally coloured.

References

Land, E.H. (1959). Experiments in color vision. *Scientific American, 200(5)*, 84–89.

——— (1977). The retinex theory of color vision. *Scientific American, 237(6)*, 108–128.

Livingstone, M.S. (1988). Art, illusion and the visual system. *Scientific American, 258(1)*, 68–75.

Walsh, V., & Kulikowski, J. (1995). Seeing colour. In R. Gregory, J. Harris, P. Heard, & Rose, D. (Eds), *The artful eye* (pp. 268–278), Oxford: Oxford University Press.

* * *

12 (a, d)   Score one point for thinking that Leon's attitude towards the workers' pay demand is likely to have become less favourable, and a second point for thinking that this would happen especially if he was paid a small amount. This surprising relationship between incentive and attitude change has been confirmed in scores of experiments based on the theory of cognitive dissonance.

The theory, which was proposed by the United States psychologist Leon Festinger in 1957, deals with the way people handle inconsistent ideas. The elements of the theory are items of knowledge or belief called cognitions. Between any pair of cognitions, one of three relations must exist. If one of the cognitions follows from the other, then the two are consonant; if one follows from the converse of the other, then they are dissonant; and if neither cognition follows from the other or from its converse, then they are irrelevant to each other. The "follows from" criterion refers to psychological rather than logical implication. Thus the two cognitions *I voted for a socialist candidate in the last election* and *I am in favour of socialism* are consonant, because the second follows psychologically from the first. This is evident from the fact that an outside observer who was informed of the first would assume that the second is more likely than its converse.

The dissonance relation, which is of special importance in the theory, is held to be a motivating state of tension, in many ways like hunger or thirst, and the theory's main assumption is that it tends to generate dissonance-reducing behaviour. Three methods of reducing dissonance are theoretically possible: changing one of the cognitions, decreasing the perceived importance of dissonant cognitions, and adding further (justifying) cognitions. The standard example of a dissonance relation is the pair of cognitions *I smoke cigarettes* and *cigarette smoking damages my health*. People who hold both of these cognitions are bound to experience dissonance, provided that they wish to be healthy – a person having a last cigarette before being executed would not necessarily experience any dissonance between the two cognitions. People can reduce the dissonance by changing the first cognition, that is, by giving up smoking or convincing themselves that they have given up when they have not really done so, but this strategy is difficult because the cognition is behaviourally anchored. Alternatively, they can change the second cognition by rejecting, ignoring, or playing down the evidence linking cigarette smoking to ill health. There is clear evidence from research that most cigarette smokers use this strategy, but it offers only limited dissonance reduction because the medical risks of smoking are so well established. The third and easiest method of reducing the dissonance is to add justifying cognitions such as *But I smoke only low-tar brands*, or *But I'm more likely to die in a car accident than from the effects of smoking*, or *But there will soon be cures for lung cancer and heart disease*, or *But I'd rather have a short, happy life than a long, miserable one*, or perhaps even *But giving up smoking won't make my life longer, it will just make it feel longer*.

In spite of its deceptive simplicity, cognitive dissonance theory generates non-obvious or counter-intuitive predictions across a wide range of human behaviour. The psychological effects of making free choices, resisting temptations, and telling lies have been studied, and findings have generally corroborated predictions from the theory. Even the behaviour of end-of-the-world cultists after their prophecies have failed have been illuminated by the theory.

In 1959 Festinger and Carlsmith reported the results of an experiment on lying from which Question 12 was developed. Students were offered either a small or a large financial reward for telling other students that some boring, repetitive tasks that they had just performed were interesting. Those who were given a small reward for telling these lies, and who therefore had the least financial justification for the dissonance between their private opinion and public declaration, came to believe what they had said (that the tasks were interesting) more than those who were given a large reward and therefore had the strongest dissonance-reducing justification for their lies. Numerous later experiments confirmed this surprising prediction from cognitive dissonance theory that attitudes change most when incentives are smallest.

Applying the theory to the specific situation described in the question, Leon's two dissonant cognitions are *I think the pay demand is reasonable* and *I told the workers that the pay demand is unreasonable*. The second cognition is behaviourally anchored and cannot be changed, but Leon can easily change the first cognition to reduce the dissonance. He can simply alter his attitude towards the reasonableness of the pay demand to make it more consonant with his public declaration to the workers. There is a third justifying cognition that must be taken into account: *But I was paid a small/large amount of money for speaking to the workers*. Its effectiveness as a justification depends on the size of the payment. If the payment was small, then the justification is weak and the drive to change the first cognition remains strong. But if the payment and therefore also the justification was large, then the need to change the first cognition is considerably less. Common sense predicts that Leon's attitude would be more likely to change if he was paid a large amount, but cognitive dissonance theory, backed up by scores of experiments, shows that the reverse is true.

References

Aronson, E. (1992). The return of the repressed: Dissonance theory makes a comeback. *Psychological Inquiry, 3*, 303–311.

Festinger, L. (1957). *A theory of cognitive dissonance*. Evanston, IL: Row, Peterson.

Festinger, L., & Carlsmith, L.M. (1959). Cognitive consequences of forced compliance. *Journal of Abnormal and Social Psychology, 58*, 203–210.

*   *   *

13 (c, f)   Score one point for realizing that most people would have remembered about the same number of nonsense syllables, and another for deciding that they would also have remembered about the same number of meaningful items. These findings are firmly established in the classical tradition of memory research, and they contradict widespread misconceptions about what it means to have a "good memory" and about the connection between ease of learning and ease of remembering.

The systematic study of memory was pioneered by the German psychologist Hermann Ebbinghaus in the 1880s. Ebbinghaus began experimenting with fragments of poetry but found that they aroused all sorts of mental associations that influenced the ease or difficulty of committing them to memory. He cast about for some kind of material that was relatively homogeneous, evoked few mental associations, and could easily be broken into objectively equal units suitable for quantitative research. He eventually hit upon the idea of the nonsense syllable, perhaps the only invention in modern history specifically designed to be as boring and meaningless as possible. Nonsense syllables are simply consonant-vowel-consonant combinations, and they are often called CVC

trigrams nowadays. With Teutonic thoroughness, Ebbinghaus pursued his research by committing several lists of nonsense syllables to memory every week throughout a significant portion of his adult life. Nonsense syllables are still used in memory research, but meaningful material is more common.

Three main factors have been found to affect the ease and speed of learning in experiments. The first is the person's learning ability: some people learn all kinds of material much more quickly than others. The second is the meaningfulness of the material: nonsense syllables are much harder to learn than meaningful words. The third is inter-item similarity: a list of very similar words or nonsense syllables tends to cause confusion and is harder to learn than a list of sharply distinctive items.

Turning now to the forgetting phase, two unexpected findings must be mentioned. First, material that is difficult to learn is remembered equally as well as material that is easy to learn, provided that both kinds are learned to the same level in the first place. Given equal time for study, difficult material will of course be retained less well, but experiments have shown that this is due entirely to the fact that it less well learned. What is important is the degree of learning, and lists of words, names, nonsense syllables, telephone numbers, or chemical formulae all show the same rate of memory decay after they have been learned to the same level. The second surprising finding is that slow learners do not forget more rapidly than quick learners. By definition, they need more time to learn material to a specified level, but having reached that level, people of about the same age forget at roughly the same rate. For example, in the experiments described in the question, young adults would forget roughly 20 per cent of the items in 24 hours, and older people would forget slightly more. This applies to material learned just sufficiently to achieve one perfect recall, as described in the question.

It is possible to go on learning beyond that point, and such over-learning, if pursued diligently enough, can reduce the forgetting rate to almost zero. Learning several lists of similar material increases the standard rate of forgetting, because items learned earlier interfere with the recall of later items (this is called proactive interference or inhibition), and items learned later interfere with recall of earlier ones (retroactive interference). Some psychologists believe that proactive and retroactive interference account for all forgetting. The reason for memory decline with age might be the accumulation of potentially interfering material throughout the lifespan.

References

Baddeley, A. (1996). *Your memory: A user's guide* (2nd ed.). London: Prion.

Ceraso, J. (1967). *Interference theory of forgetting.* San Francisco, CA: W.H. Freeman.

Ebbinghaus, H. (1913). *Memory* (Trans. H. Ruyer & C.E. Bussenius). New York: Teachers College, Columbia University. (Original work published 1885)

* * *

14 (b)   Score one point for supposing that the second rat displayed the habit for longer than the first. This finding has been replicated hundreds of times in experiments on *instrumental conditioning*

involving *reinforcement schedules*. Instrumental or operant conditioning is a type of learning studied since the 1930s by the United
States psychologist Burrhus F. Skinner (1904–1990) and his
followers. It is more readily applicable than the process of classical
conditioning discovered by the Nobel prize-winning Russian physiologist Ivan P. Pavlov (1849–1936). In the jargon of modern
learning theory, the rats referred to in the question were conditioned
in a Skinner box, the lever-pressing response was reinforced with
food pellets, a continuous schedule of reinforcement was used with
the first rat, and a partial schedule was used with the second.

The concepts of instrumental conditioning have been applied to
various forms of behaviour in rats, pigeons, human beings and
many other species. Its properties are now well understood, and its
effects are highly predictable, with surprisingly little variation from
one species to the next. An operant technique called shaping can be
used to train animals more effectively than any other known
method. Shaping involves gradually building up the desired pattern
of behaviour by selectively reinforcing successive approximations to
it. In one famous application of this technique, a number of pigs
were trained to turn on a radio, eat at a table, run a vacuum cleaner
over the floor, and put a pile of washing in a basket. Human beings
have been conditioned with smiles, nods, and other signs of
approval during ordinary conversations to increase the frequency
with which they give opinions, refer to themselves, or manifest some
other type of behaviour. Shaping techniques have been widely used
to modify problem behaviour among children, criminal offenders,
and mental patients. Skinner's followers believe that virtually all
behaviour can be explained in terms of instrumental conditioning
occurring naturally in everyday life, although this view has been
challenged by non-behaviourists, especially following the work of
the United States linguist Noam Chomsky in the 1960s showing
that conditioning cannot satisfactorily explain the learning and use
of language.

Continuous and partial reinforcement schedules produce strik-
ingly different patterns of behaviour, and different partial schedules
have different effects. The experiments described in the question
involved a continuous schedule in the first case and a partial
schedule in the second. The partial schedule used in the second case
was what is called a variable-ratio schedule, because the animal was
reinforced after irregular numbers of lever presses, in other words
the ratio of reinforcements to lever presses was variable. This type

of schedule produces extremely persistent behaviour patterns. An animal trained on a variable-ratio schedule of reinforcement will typically expend more energy making the responses than it gets back in food reinforcements. A human equivalent is gambling. Many people display remarkably persistent behaviour patterns that guarantee a net loss in the long run when confronted with one-armed bandits, fruit machines, or other gambling devices, no doubt because gambling involves a variable-ratio schedule of reinforcement. The most striking feature of partial reinforcement schedules in general and variable-ratio schedules in particular is that the behaviour they generate persists for a very long time after the reinforcements are withdrawn. Habits acquired through continuous schedules of reinforcement die away much more quickly in the absence of reinforcement. These well-established findings provide the answer to the question.

References

Ferster, C.B., & Skinner, B.F. (1957). *Schedules of reinforcement.* New York: Appleton-Century-Crofts.

Mackintosh, N.J. (1983). *Conditioning and associative learning.* Oxford: Oxford University Press.

Skinner, B.F. (1974). *About behaviorism.* New York: Alfred A. Knopf.

Smith, T.L. (1994). *Behavior and its causes: Philosophical foundations of operant psychology.* Dordrecht: Kluwer Academic.

* * *

15 (b) Score one point. Exceptionally intelligent people are in general physically and mentally healthier than others. The evidence for this comes from various sources including a continuing study initiated by the United States psychologist Lewis Terman in the early 1920s of 1470 exceptionally intelligent children.

Terman's gifted sample, who often referred to themselves as the "Termites", were selected from the Californian school system in 1921. All had IQs above 135, which puts them in the top 1 per cent of the population intellectually. Their ages at the beginning of the study ranged from 3 to 19 years. They were assessed on a variety of psychological tests and were also examined physically.

The gifted sample turned out to be untypical of the general population in several ways apart from intelligence. No fewer than

10.5 per cent of the Termites, and 17 per cent of those who were later most successful in their careers, were Jewish, compared to an estimated 5 per cent of Jews in the population from which they were selected. Roughly one-third came from professional families, although only 3 per cent of the population belonged to that social class in 1921.

The Termites were tested and interviewed in 1922, 1928, 1940, 1950, 1955, 1960, 1972, 1982 and 1992. Some died and the researchers lost contact with others along the way, but approximately half the original sample was still available for the 1992 follow-up. The results of the first 35 years of the investigation are contained in the five volumes of Terman's *Genetic Studies of Genius*. After Terman's death in 1956 the project was carried on by others. Among the younger researchers who took over control of the project was Robert Sears, a well-known professor of psychology who later revealed that he was himself a member of the original sample of Termites. Although the study has been criticized on various grounds, the findings regarding physical and mental health have not been challenged and have been corroborated by other research studies.

When they were children, the Termites were found to be generally above average on a wide variety of measures related to physical and mental health. They were not intellectually one-sided, emotionally unstable, or socially unpopular, nor did they show any other types of maladjustment. On almost every personality and character trait they scored better than the general school population. A high proportion, though not as many as might have been expected, turned out to be highly successful in their careers. Their occupations ranged from sandwich-shop attendant to university professor. Their average income in adult life has been about four times the national average. The female Termites were ahead of their time in adopting ideas and lifestyles that became fashionable later. Compared with other women of their generation, they tended to marry later, have fewer children, and produce them later in life, and they were more likely to remain single. Most of them followed careers of one sort or another, and they were generally happier in their work than other women, perhaps because they tended to get better jobs. The physical and mental health of the Termites, both male and female, has remained good to very good compared with the rest of the population.

Terman summarized his results as follows:

It is to be hoped that the superstitions so commonly accepted relative to the intellectually superior children have been permanently swept away by the factual data these studies have presented. It is simply not true that such children are especially prone to be puny, over-specialized in their abilities and interests, emotionally unstable, socially unadaptable, psychotic, and morally undependable; nor is it true that they usually deteriorate to the level of mediocrity as adult life is approached.

(Terman, 1943, p. 305)

References

Holahan, C.K., Sears, R.R., & Cronbach, L.J. (1995). *The gifted group in later maturity*. Stanford, CA: Stanford University Press.

Shurkin, J.N. (1992). *Terman's kids: The groundbreaking study of how the gifted grew up*. Boston, MA: Little, Brown.

Subotnik, R.F., & Arnold, K.D. (Eds) (1994). *Beyond Terman: Contemporary longitudinal studies of giftedness and talent*. Norwood, NJ: Ablex.

Terman, L.M. (Ed.) (1925–1959). *Genetic studies of genius* (Vols I–V). Stanford, CA: Stanford University Press.

Terman, L.M. (1943) 'Mental and physical traits of a thousand gifted children.' In R.G. Baker, J.S. Kounin, & H.F. Wright (Eds) *Child behavior and development* (pp. 279–306). New York: McGraw Hill.

* * *

16 (a)   Score one point for supposing that schizophrenia is more common among unskilled working-class people than among the upper middle class, and a bonus point for stating the reverse relationship between social class and autistic disorder (autism).

In 1958 a carefully controlled survey by Hollingshead and Redlich in New Haven, Connecticut reported that the prevalence of schizophrenia – the total number of cases of schizophrenia as a proportion of the population – was more than eight times as high in unskilled working-class families than in professional and managerial families. Later studies in the United States and other industrial societies have generally confirmed this finding, though not the exact figure. For example, in 1991 Robins and Regier reported the results of the largest United States study of mental illness to date, a survey of 20,000 people in five states, and their data showed the prevalence of schizophrenia to be five times as high in the lowest social class as in the highest. But although the finding is well established, its explanation remains obscure and controversial.

Some authorities have argued that the class difference may be due to a bias of diagnosis, reflecting a reluctance on the part of psychiatrists and clinical psychologists to attach the label of schizophrenia to patients of high socio-economic status or an over-eagerness to attach it to people of low status. This explanation has been thrown into doubt by census studies, based on objective examinations of whole communities rather than possibly biased samples of people already diagnosed as having schizophrenia, in which the class difference has remained. The supposed social bias in diagnosis is also difficult to reconcile with the fact that some equally unpleasant disorders such as autistic disorder are more prevalent in upper-middle-class families, and that others such as bipolar disorder (manic–depressive disorder) show no strong or consistent social class differences. If psychiatrists are more willing to diagnose patients of low socio-economic status with schizophrenia, why are they not equally biased when it comes to these other disorders?

A different kind of explanation focuses on psychological stress factors. The assumption is that certain unspecified aspects of child-rearing or everyday life in poor families create stresses that put people at risk of developing schizophrenia. This suggestion is weakened by the inability of researchers to isolate the particular stress factors that are supposedly involved in the production or causation of schizophrenia.

The social drift theory proposes that people with schizophrenia are unable to hold on to middle-class jobs and tend therefore to drift downwards through the social class hierarchy and accumulate at the lowest levels. The main weakness of this explanation is that although it can explain the higher *prevalence* of schizophrenia at the lowest class levels, research has also established that there is a significantly higher *incidence* – proportion of new cases – originating in the lowest class levels, and the social drift theory is powerless to explain this. Most studies, in any case, have failed to find evidence of sufficient downward drift to account for the massive class differences. A refined version of this theory has therefore been put forward in terms of social residue rather than social drift. According to the social residue hypothesis, people with schizophrenia may or may not drift downwards, but they are less likely to rise upwards through the class system than other people, even before their symptoms have become severe. This could explain the disproportionately high prevalence and incidence of the disorder at the lowest class levels.

Children with autistic disorder display emotional non-responsiveness, lack of reciprocity in social interaction, failure to develop peer relations, delay or failure of speech development, stereotyped and idiosyncratic language usage or non-verbal behaviour, including eye-contact avoidance, insistence on sameness, and ritualized mannerisms. Ever since the disorder was first described by Leo Kanner in 1943 psychiatrists and clinical psychologists have suspected that it is more prevalent in upper-middle-class than working-class families, and careful research has generally confirmed this suspicion. No entirely persuasive explanation for this class bias has been suggested.

References

Hollingshead, A.B., & Redlich, F.C. (1958). *Social class and mental illness: A community study*. New York: Wiley.

Robins, L.N., & Regier, D.A. (Eds.) (1991). *Psychiatric disorders in America: The epidemiologic catchment area study*. New York: Free Press.

Schreibman, L. (1988). *Autism*. Newbury Park, CA: Sage.

* * *

17 (c)   Score one point. Multiple or split personality is classified as a dissociative identity disorder. It is characterized by the presence of two or more separate personalities, each with its own memories and patterns of behaviour, that recurrently take control of behaviour. It is quite unrelated to schizophrenia, or to bipolar disorder (manic–depressive disorder), which is one of the mood disorders (see chapter 3).

The widespread confusion of multiple personality with schizophrenia probably arises from the derivation of its name. The name *schizophrenia* was coined by the Swiss psychiatrist Eugen Bleuler in 1911 from the Greek words *schizein* (to split) and *phren* (mind, originally midriff, supposed at one time to be the seat of the soul). It denotes a type of disorder involving a lack of connection between thought processes, emotions, and behaviour, or a splitting up or disintegration of psychological functions rather than a cleaving in two. The splitting implied by the word has nothing whatever to do with the alternation between different personalities found in dissociative identity disorder. The hallmarks of schizophrenia are symptoms such as false beliefs maintained in the face of overwhelming contradictory evidence (delusions), perceptions of people or things that are not present (hallucinations), disorganized speech and behaviour, emotional flattening, inability to initiate or sustain purposeful activities, and marked deterioration in work, social relations, and self-care.

Schizophrenia is a relatively common disorder, occurring with a lifetime prevalence of about 1 per cent in most industrial countries in which surveys have been conducted. Multiple personality disorder is a very rare and controversial condition. It is related to dissociative amnesia, a disorder characterized by loss of memory, usually for important recent events associated with personal problems, stress, or unexpected bereavement; to dissociative fugue, characterized by sudden unexpected travel away from home, amnesia for some or all of the past, and confusion about personal identity or the assumption of a new identity; and to dissociative movement disorders in which there is a partial or complete loss of ability to perform bodily movements that are normally under voluntary control.

References

American Psychiatric Association. (1994). *Diagnostic and statistical manual of mental disorders* (4th ed.). Washington, DC: Author.

Freeman, C.P.L. (1993). Neurotic disorders. In R.E. Kendell, & A.K. Zealley (Eds), *Companion to psychiatric studies* (5th ed., pp. 485–524), Edinburgh: Churchill Livingstone.

Kendell, R.E. (1993). Schizophrenia. In R.E. Kendell, & A.K. Zealley (Eds), *Companion to psychiatric studies* (5th ed., pp. 397–426), Edinburgh: Churchill Livingstone.

* * *

18 (b) Score one point. The group decisions are likely to have been riskier than the average of the individual decisions. This is an example of the group polarization phenomenon. Although the phenomenon is strongly counter-intuitive, it is robust and easily exhibited in classroom demonstrations.

A special case of group polarization, called the risky shift, was discovered independently in the United States by a psychologist called Edward Ziller in 1957 and a graduate student called James Stoner in 1961. Using quite different methods, both researchers showed that, for decisions involving risk, group decisions tend to be riskier than individual decisions. Both were surprised by their findings, because intuition suggests that committees, boards, councils, and other decision making bodies tend to temper individual recklessness and to stifle boldness and daring. But scores of experiments in laboratories and naturalistic field settings have confirmed the original finding that, for most kinds of dilemmas involving risk, group decisions tend to be riskier than individual decisions, although there are exceptions. The well-known tendency in labour disputes for mass meetings to produce more militant decisions than secret ballots is due, in part at least, to this phenomenon. Gambling decisions, such as those described in the question, invariably conform to the risky shift.

In 1969 the French psychologists Moscovici and Zavalloni discovered a more general effect in group decision making that they called the group polarization phenomenon. This is a tendency for group decisions, including those that do not involve risk, to amplify the predominant individual opinions of the group members. The French researchers showed that the generally favourable attitudes of students towards de Gaulle became even more positive, and their generally unfavourable attitudes towards Americans became even more negative, following group discussion. This general effect was confirmed by investigators in many parts of the world, and by the mid 1970s it had become apparent that the risky shift was merely a special case of the group polarization phenomenon. In decisions involving risk, the risky shift occurs if the individual opinions of the group members incline towards the risky end of the risk–caution spectrum, and individual opinions are usually biased in this direction because of cultural bias favouring risk taking over caution. In such cases, the effect of the group discussion is to amplify the predominant individual inclination to risk.

Several hypotheses or theories have been suggested to explain the group polarization phenomenon. The two most satisfactory theories are based on similar assumptions. In decisions involving risk the social comparison theory assumes that, in a western industrial cultures, people in general tend to admire riskiness rather than caution and therefore like to consider themselves at least as willing to take risks as their peers. During the group discussion, some of the group members are likely to discover that there are others present whose individual decisions are riskier than their own. To restore their self-images, they therefore alter their decisions in the direction of greater risk taking, and this shifts the group decision in a risky direction. The persuasive argumentation theory rests on the assumption that, because people tend to admire riskiness rather than caution, persuasive arguments in favour of risk are more likely to be voiced during the group discussions than are arguments in favour of caution, and people are therefore more likely to be persuaded to change their opinions in a risky direction.

The social comparison and persuasive argumentation theories are both powerful and can be applied, with minor modifications, to group decisions of all kinds, whether they involve risk or not. For example, they can explain Moscovici and Zavalloni's finding that French students' favourable opinions of de Gaulle became more favourable and their unfavourable opinions of Americans became more unfavourable after group discussions. The assumptions behind the theories have been carefully tested by experimenters, and they have been strongly confirmed. The phenomenon of group polarization is reasonably well understood, and there is evidence to suggest that it results from both social comparison and persuasive argumentation effects.

References

Bar-Nir, A. (1998). Can group- and issue-related factors predict choice shift? A meta-analysis of group decisions on life dilemmas. *Small Group Research, 29*, 308–338.

Isenberg, D.J. (1986). Group polarization: A critical review and meta-analysis. *Journal of Personality and Social Psychology, 50*, 1141–1151.

Liu, J.H., & Latané, B. (1998). Extremitization of attitudes: Does thought- and discussion-induced polarization cumulate? *Basic and Applied Social Psychology, 20*, 103–110.

Myers, D.G., & Lamm, H. (1976). The group polarization phenomenon. *Psychological Bulletin, 83*, 602–627.

*   *   *

19 (a)   Score one point for identifying prohibition of sex between certain close relatives as the only one of the listed options that is common to all known human societies.

The rules and conventions governing sex and marriage show a surprising amount of variation from one society to the next. In Tibet it is quite common for several brothers to share the same wife. Among the Sotho tribesmen of southern Africa, and in many other tribal societies, a positive obligation exists to marry a cross-cousin – a child of one's mother's brother or father's sister – if it is possible to do so. The Pondo people of the Transkei have a strict set of taboos governing name avoidance by married women. A Pondo bride is forbidden in ordinary conversation to utter the names of her husband's elder brothers, her father-in-law or his brothers, or her husband's paternal grandfather, whether they are living or dead, and she is not even allowed to use words that rhyme with any of these names – a Pondo bride needs a high level of verbal dexterity! But in spite of the striking differences in sex and marriage customs, all of these societies, and all others that have ever been investigated, share one type of rule in common: they all prohibit sex and marriage between certain members (usually between all members) of the nuclear family, the primary family unit of father, mother, and children. This prohibition is called the incest taboo.

Psychologists, sociologists, sociobiologists, and social anthropologists have suggested numerous possible explanations for the culturally universal incest taboo. Sociologists have suggested that it serves the function of creating and maintaining important networks of social relationships without which societies would disintegrate into separate family units. The assumption is that societies without incest taboos have been eliminated by natural selection. This functional theory rests on the controversial assumption that if it were not for the incest taboo, everyone would naturally want to mate with and marry a close relative. It also fails to explain why there is a taboo on sexual intercourse with close relatives rather than merely a taboo on marriage.

A different but related theory rests on genetic assumptions. According to some sociobiologists, inbreeding would in the long run lead to the genetic deterioration and ultimate extinction of any society that practised it, because harmful recessive genes would be more likely to come together, and the incest taboo is alleged to have evolved by a similar kind of natural selection to that proposed by the functionalists. The assumption is based on well-established biological facts, but it lacks persuasive force none the less. It leaves open the question as to why most non-human animals have not evolved incest taboos – although ethologists have shown that all primates do avoid incest – and it is severely embarrassed by the existence of many societies, like the Sotho people mentioned earlier, in which there is a positive obligation of marriage between cross-cousins, who share one-eighth of their genes in common. Both the functional and the genetic theories lack a psychological dimension. Even if we grant the dire sociological or biological consequences of widespread incest, the problem remains of explaining why individual members of a society generally refrain from committing incest although they have not read the sociology and biology textbooks.

The most satisfactory psychological theory, popularized by the Swedish philosopher Edward Westermarck in 1894, rests on the assumption that intimate contact between children at a critical period before puberty (now believed to be between 2 and 6 years of age), such as occurs in the nuclear family, results in a lack of sexual attraction between them in adult life. The crucial assumption behind this pre-pubertal interaction theory is strongly supported by evidence from Israeli kibbutzim. These communal farms are organized in such a way that contact between unrelated children is as intimate as that between siblings, and although most parents would like their offspring to marry within the kibbutz, virtually all marriages turn out to be between members of different kibbutzim.

In spite of the taboo, incest does occur from time to time in all societies, and this also needs to be explained. The pre-pubertal interaction theory can explain it rather neatly. Household arrangements in some societies, including our own, occasionally involve a lack of intimate contact between siblings when they are young, and between children and their parents. Even institutionalized incest, in the form of brother–sister marriages among royalty in ancient Egypt and elsewhere, may be explicable, at least in part, by a lack of pre-pubertal interaction in large royal households in which children are raised by servants and have little or no intimate contact with their siblings and parents.

Astonishingly, a knowledge of the connection between sexual intercourse and pregnancy is not universal. During the First World War, the Polish social anthropologist Bronislaw Malinowski discovered a society in north-western Melanesia in which this simple fact was obviously unknown. Later investigators have confirmed that these people, the Trobriand Islanders of Papua New Guinea, continue to this day to deny dogmatically that there is any connection between sexual intercourse and pregnancy, in spite of strenuous efforts by missionaries and others to explain the facts of life to them. Pig farming, which is a vital part of Trobriand food production, is severely hampered by their ignorance, because the Trobriand Islanders believe that sows fall pregnant for reasons unrelated to sexual intercourse.

According to the Trobriand Islanders, a woman conceives after one of the spirits of her dead relatives touches her forehead while she sleeps. Blood rushes to her head and carries the spirit-child to her womb. The blood continues to nourish the foetus after conception, which is why menstruation ceases when she becomes pregnant. The suggestion that sexual intercourse causes pregnancy is regarded by the Trobriand Islanders as ignorant and absurd. Facial resemblances between fathers and their children are explained by the notion that a man's features can be imprinted on an unborn spirit-child's face during sexual intercourse with the mother while she is pregnant. Various arguments and evidence are produced to refute the sexual intercourse theory. For example, Malinowski was told of a blind and feeble-minded Trobriand woman with a hideous face and deformed body who was so grotesquely unattractive that no man could possibly bring himself to have intercourse with her. Yet she had a child, the natives triumphantly pointed out whenever Malinowski raised the topic of sexual intercourse and pregnancy. Another popular argument among the Trobriand Islanders was that many women never have children in spite of being sexually promiscuous – most Trobriand girls have lost their virginity by the time they are 8 years old, and of course contraceptive methods are not practised. One informant told Malinowski how he had once returned home after an absence of two years and was delighted to find his wife with a new-born baby. He volunteered this information as final proof that sexual intercourse can have nothing to do with pregnancy.

The evidence regarding homosexuality can be dealt with briefly. Many societies have been found in which homosexuality is tolerated, approved of, or even considered obligatory. For example, among the Keraki of New Guinea and the aboriginal Aranda people of south central Australia, male adolescents are expected to take part in anal intercourse with male partners for a full year after initiation, and this is followed by a long period of active homosexuality before they are considered to be ready for heterosexual marriage. About 64 per cent of societies for which evidence is available consider homosexuality acceptable for at least some of the people some of the time. A few, such as the Etero and Marind-Anim of New Guinea, are primarily homosexual, but these societies have difficulty maintaining their population numbers.

References

Ford, C.S., & Beach, F.A. (1951). *Patterns of sexual behavior.* New York: Harper.

Fox, R. (1983). *Kinship and marriage: An anthropological perspective* (2nd ed.). Cambridge: Cambridge University Press.

Malinowski, B. (1932). *The sexual life of savages in north-western Melanesia* (3rd ed.). London: Routledge & Kegan Paul.

van den Berghe, P.L. (1983). Human inbreeding avoidance: Culture in nature. *The Behavioral and Brain Sciences, 6,* 91–123.

* * *

20 (e) Score one point for thinking that Bibb and the others would probably have failed to report the fire in time. You may be surprised to learn that people are much less likely to intervene in an emergency, and generally slower to respond, when other people are present than when they are alone. The emergency described in the question closely resembles the situation created in a classic experiment on bystander intervention by the United States psychologists Bibb Latané and John Darley in 1968. Of the people who were alone in the waiting-room when the smoke appeared, 55 per cent reported the fire within two minutes of first noticing it, and 75 per cent reported it within six minutes. When groups of three were tested together, in only 12 per cent of cases did *any of the three* report the fire within two minutes, and in only 38 per cent of cases within six minutes.

More than fifty experiments by dozens of independent groups of researchers have confirmed Latané and Darley's original finding that the presence of other people inhibits the impulse to help in an emergency. In one laboratory experiment people were led to believe that a bookcase had toppled on to a woman in an adjacent room, trapping her leg, and 70 per cent who were alone, but only 7 per cent accompanied by passive bystanders, went to her assistance within two minutes. In a lifelike field experiment, a theft from a liquor store in New York was repeatedly staged while either one or two customers were at the check-out counter from which they had a clear view of the crime, and 65 per cent of the solitary customers reported the theft to the cashier, but in only 56 per cent of the pairs did either of the customers report it. Other laboratory and field experiments have involved medical emergencies in which people apparently fainted, suffered asthma attacks or epileptic seizures, or injured themselves, and non-medical emergencies in which people appeared to need help because their cars had broken down, for example. With rare exceptions, both the laboratory and the field experiments have confirmed the finding that people are much less likely to intervene helpfully in emergency situations when other people are present. Overall, more than two-thirds of people tested alone but fewer than one-third of people tested in groups have helped, and the response times in groups have been much longer. The socially induced bystander apathy originally discovered by Latané and Darley is clearly a robust and remarkably consistent effect.

Why are people in groups less willing to help in emergencies and much slower to respond when they do help? Social psychologists have tackled this problem by breaking down the process of helping into its component stages. Before intervening, a person must first notice that something is happening, realize that it is an emergency, acknowledge personal responsibility for acting, decide on a suitable form of assistance, and finally implement the assistance. This analysis suggests three psychological factors that might explain the socially induced inhibition of helping. The first is called audience inhibition: the presence of other people may inhibit helping in so far as an attempt to intervene may lead to embarrassment if it turns out that what seemed to be an emergency was not an emergency after all. Second, social influence can inhibit helping, because emergencies tend to be more or less ambiguous, and the presence of other passive bystanders can encourage people to interpret such a situation as less critical than it might otherwise appear to be. The third psychological factor is called diffusion of responsibility. When other people are present, people are less likely to feel individually responsible for giving assistance and more likely to assume that they cannot be held personally accountable for failing to intervene, because everyone present would be equally culpable.

References

Dovidio, J.F. (1984). Helping behavior and altruism: An empirical and conceptual overview. In L. Berkowitz (Ed.), *Advances in experimental social psychology* (Vol. 17, pp. 361–427), New York: Academic Press.

Latané, B., & Darley, J.M. (1970). *The unresponsive bystander: Why doesn't he help?* New York: Appleton-Century-Crofts.

Latané, B., & Naida, S. (1981). Ten years of research on group size and helping. *Psychological Bulletin, 89*, 308–324.

Piliavin, J.A., Dovidio, J.F., Gaertner, S.L., & Clark, R.D. (1981). *Emergency intervention.* New York: Academic Press.

* * *

Interpretation of scores

Now add up your points. Check that you have counted perfectly correct answers only. In awarding yourself bonus points you must in some cases be trusted to use your own judgement in deciding whether your answers are correct or not.

If you have worked through the quiz patiently and studied the answers and explanations carefully, then you will have learnt quite a lot about the nature and scope of psychology. If you used to believe that psychology is nothing but common sense, you have probably changed your mind by now. Above all, you have no doubt acquired an intuitive feel for the subject.

The quiz does not represent a perfectly balanced selection from the standard undergraduate syllabus of psychology. My choice of topics was constrained in several ways. To begin with, the questions were specifically designed to trip you up, hence most of them capitalized on research findings that are either surprising or simply unavailable to intuition. Many aspects of behaviour and mental experience are relatively transparent, and for that reason unsuitable for a deliberately tricky quiz. Second, I was restricted to research findings that lend themselves to straightforward question-and-answer presentation. I had to exclude questions that would need substantial background information to be understood, and I was unable to include psychological problems to which the answers are not clear-cut. Third, I thought it prudent to include only well-established findings that are unlikely to be challenged or overturned by future research, and one important consequence of this is that many of the problems on which the quiz is based are no longer live issues in psychology. Lastly, my own personal knowledge and interests have inevitably played a part in biasing the selection. But, bearing all these qualifications in mind, the quiz does not give too misleading an impression of the spectrum of psychological research. About three-quarters of the questions relate to topics that are dealt with in most degree courses at good universities. This does not mean that all of those questions could be answered correctly by a typical psychology graduate, because many of the questions demand a knowledge of specific topics that is more intimate and detailed than students are normally expected to acquire.

The maximum possible score is 30 points. If the quiz had been sprung on me, I think I would have scored about 25 points. A study of 250 school-leavers in England, all considering studying psychology at university and some having studied it formally at school, produced an average score equivalent to about 12 points – in fact, the average score was 39 per cent excluding bonus points (see A. Furnham, Prospective psychology students' knowledge of psychology, *Psychological Reports*, 70: 375–382, 1992). For the respondents in that study, the easiest questions, with 80 per cent or more correct answers, were Questions 12 (cognitive dissonance) and 1 (duration of dreams), and the hardest, with 5 per cent or fewer correct answers, were Questions 8 (Fechner's law) and 15 (Terman's study of giftedness). What follows is an interpretation of scores that should not be taken too seriously.

Score	Interpretation
0–7	You were guessing, and you have little or no specialized knowledge of psychology. On the other hand, the fact that you completed the quiz suggests that you have enough interest, motivation, and patience to become an expert if you decide to put your mind to it.
8–12	Either you were guessing very cleverly, or you have some knowledge of psychology, or (most likely) both.
13–17	You have read and understood a wide range of psychological literature, and you have some aptitude for the subject.
18–22	You have reached the level of a good psychology graduate.
23–27	You are a competent psychologist who keeps up with the technical literature in a wide range of areas.
28–30	You are a shameless cheat! You will probably go far in any walk of life.

Chapter 3

The subject matter of psychology

The number of students enrolled in psychology courses has been increasing steadily for several decades in the United Kingdom, the United States, and most other western industrial nations, and the number of female psychology students has been growing especially fast. In 1970, the proportion of female first degree graduates in psychology was marginally below 50 per cent in the United Kingdom and marginally above 50 per cent in the United States, but by the late 1990s it had increased to approximately 75 per cent in both countries, and something similar has occurred in other western European countries and in countries such as Australia and South Africa. The annual number of psychology graduates in the United Kingdom has increased from less than 200 in 1960 to about 6000 in the late 1990s. Psychology was introduced as an independently examined school subject in the United Kingdom in 1970, and by the late 1990s some 30,000 school pupils were sitting psychology A level examinations every year. In the United States, more than 10 per cent of college and university students choose psychology, and in opinion surveys about 70 per cent say they would do so again. A United States psychologist once commented that God must love psychology students, because He created so many of them.

The popularity of psychology has relatively little to do with career prospects, which I shall examine in chapter 6. By far the most common reason that students give for choosing psychology is interest in its subject matter. Surveys have shown that schoolchildren tend to have a vague and distorted image of psychology, and a majority of them confuse psychology with psychoanalysis and psychiatry, but at least they know that it is concerned largely with people. It is natural and proper for people to be interested in themselves and in other members of their own species, and it would therefore be surprising if psychology were not a popular subject. What do psychology students learn? I have discussed the nature of the subject and some of its boundaries in chapter 1, and I have illustrated it with concrete examples in chapter 2. The aim of this chapter is to outline its subject matter.

A formal education in psychology teaches two things, a body of specialized information and a set of skills. In the long run, the skills are probably more important than the information, because information is stored in libraries and on the Internet where it is always available to be looked up, whereas skills have to be carried around in our skulls. Students of psychology probably learn a wider range of skills than students of any other subject. The reason for this is the unique diversity of its subject matter, which reflects the fact that psychology straddles the arts, sciences, and social sciences.

Perhaps the most useful intellectual skills that psychologists learn are problem-solving techniques. Long after they have forgotten most of the facts that they learnt as students, psychologists usually retain skills that enable them to approach new problems in fruitful ways. Psychology students learn to locate information in libraries and on the Internet and to evaluate controversial ideas critically. They are trained to devise techniques for measuring attitudes, opinions, and various types of behaviour. They learn the fundamental ideas behind statistics, including methods of interpreting numerical data to determine objectively whether an effect is significant or should be attributed to chance, and they usually acquire a range of skills associated with information technology, including the ability to analyse data on computers. They are taught the basic principles of behaviour modification and the most effective methods of altering behaviour patterns in other people and themselves. They are trained to express themselves orally and in writing, and to listen attentively to other people. After studying a relatively young and rapidly changing subject, they are well-practised at entertaining new ideas and making sense of controversies. Above all, they are equipped to devise scientific methods for answering many kinds of empirical questions. The literacy, numeracy, interpersonal, technical, and practical skills that psychologists acquire as part of their basic education are likely to be useful to them in later life, whether they follow careers in psychology or not.

Basic research and applied psychology

The fundamental goal of psychology can be stated quite simply: it is to understand the nature, functions, and phenomena of behaviour and mental experience. The examples given in chapter 2 illustrate how problems arise in explaining behavioural and mental phenomena and how empirical research can sometimes help to solve them. Like any other branch of science, psychology aims to enlarge our understanding of the world. What distinguishes it from other scientific disciplines is the class of problems with which it deals. Basic research psychologists, like basic researchers in other fields, regard understanding and explanation as ends in themselves. A research contribution is considered important if it throws light on an aspect of behaviour or mental experience that was not previously well understood; its value is not measured according to its immediate or potential usefulness for solving *practical* problems. But a great deal of psychology *is* meant to be useful, and the various fields of applied psychology discussed in chapter 6 have essentially pragmatic or utilitarian aims.

There is considerable controversy over the issue of practical usefulness in psychology, and it is worth pausing to examine it more closely. Many people regard research that offers no prospect of practical usefulness as futile or pointless, and government agencies that provide the funds for research are sometimes accused of sharing that view. But many psychologists who devote their lives to basic research regard it as a philistine opinion. The key question is whether or not it is worthwhile carrying out research solely to find things out. There are some who think it shocking that the question is even asked. Curiosity is a natural human instinct and it seems self-evident that we should try to learn as much as possible about the world we live in, whether or not the research is likely to be useful in any practical sense. Our culture is enriched when archaeologists discover something new about ancient civilizations, when astronomers solve mysteries about distant objects in the universe, and when mathematicians prove theorems about arcane mathematical entities. Basic research in archaeology, astronomy, and mathematics needs no justification in a civilized society, and the same can be said of basic research in psychology and other subjects. In any event, what is the criterion of practical usefulness? Surely something is practically useful if it increases human happiness? If so, then fine art, literature, and music are among the most directly useful subjects, and sports and pastimes are at least as useful as engineering, business studies, and law.

But basic research does not cover the whole of psychology. The various fields of applied psychology are concerned with applications of psychology to practical problems of life, rather than to theoretical problems of understanding and explanation. Applied psychology relies partly on the findings of basic research, in so far as these findings are relevant to the practical problems in hand, and partly on investigations specifically designed to provide solutions to the practical problems. In clinical and counselling psychology, research into mental disorders is applied with the ultimate aim of helping people with those disorders. In educational and school psychology, research into problems of learning, adjustment, and behaviour among schoolchildren is applied in an effort to provide practical help to children, their parents, and their teachers. In occupational and industrial/organizational psychology, the results of basic and applied research into the well-being and efficiency of people in work is applied to problems arising in the workplace and more generally in organizations. And in forensic and criminological psychology problems associated with criminal behaviour, criminal investigation, and legal processes in court are addressed. I shall discuss these and other areas of applied psychology in more detail in chapter 6, which is about psychology as a profession. The rest of this chapter will be devoted to outlining the main areas of psychological research that are taught in universities and colleges.

Main areas of psychological research

There are many different ways of classifying psychological research. Early textbooks often divided psychology up into schools – structuralist, functionalist, behaviourist, Gestalt, and psychoanalytic – but this criterion of classification lost most of its relevance after the decline of the schools in the 1930s and 1940s (see chapter 5). There are several different classifications that focus on the types of organisms under investigation, dividing psychology up into child psychology and adult psychology, or into human psychology and animal psychology, or into general psychology and abnormal psychology, for example. Some classifications are based on the research methods that are used – experimental psychology, qualitative psychology, mathematical psychology, and so forth. All classifications are arbitrary and conjectural. The Argentine story-teller Jorge Luis Borges illustrated this point nicely when he described an apocryphal Chinese encyclopedia in which animals were divided into:

(a) those that belong to the Emperor, (b) embalmed ones, (c) those that are trained, (d) suckling pigs, (e) mermaids, (f) fabulous ones, (g) stray dogs, (h) those that are included in this classification, (i) those that tremble as if they were mad, (j) innumerable ones, (k) those drawn with a very fine camel's hair brush, (l) others, (m) those that have just broken a flower vase, (n) those that resemble flies from a distance. (Borges, J.L., 1973, *Other inquisitions, 1937–1952*, R.L.C. Simms, Trans., London: Souvenir, p. 103, original work published 1952)

The conventional classification of psychological research that has grown up by custom and practice is a mongrel system, almost as chaotic and ambiguous as the Chinese encyclopedia, based partly on categories of psychological processes (sensation and perception, cognition, learning and skills, emotion and motivation, individual differences and personality, social psychology), partly on levels of analysis (biological aspects of behaviour, developmental psychology, history of psychology), and partly on the types of individuals under investigation (abnormal psychology, comparative psychology). Unsurprisingly, this system is difficult to apply in practice. Psychological processes, and to an extent also levels of analysis and types of individuals, stubbornly refuse to be confined in watertight compartments. A certain leakage between categories is inevitable, and new phenomena and research areas that do not seem to belong in any of the existing pigeon-holes keep turning up. As a result, the same basic body of information tends to be organized and divided up slightly differently from one textbook or course outline to the next.

The system of classification that is set out below is not necessarily more logical than any other, but it corresponds as closely as possible to the way the discipline is divided up for teaching purposes in degree courses in the United States and the United Kingdom, according to published surveys that I have examined and distilled. The eleven research categories that follow will give you a bird's-eye view of the subject matter of contemporary psychology as it is taught in leading universities. The brief notes about specific topics within the general categories are merely illustrative and are meant to convey only a flavour of the kinds of material generally included.

I *Biological aspects of behaviour* (Questions 1, 2, 3, and 9 ... ...c quiz in chapter 2 belong wholly or partly in this category.) This category is often (tendentiously, in my opinion) called the biological bases of behaviour. Major topics within it include human heredity and behaviour genetics, comparative psychology and the evolution of behaviour, the central nervous system including the anatomy and physiology of the brain, brain imaging, physiological psychology, neuropsychology, the autonomic nervous system, the endocrine system, states of consciousness including sleep and dreaming, and the psychological effects of drugs. What follows are a few sketchy notes on these topics.

Genetic factors, which were first investigated by an Austrian monk called Gregor Mendel in 1865, play an important role in the development of behaviour. Every cell in the human body apart from the sex cells carries twenty-three pairs of chromosomes, and the sex cells carry just one member of each pair. Each chromosome contains a tightly coiled molecule of deoxyribonucleic acid (DNA) that stores the hereditary code in about 100,000 units called genes encoded in 3 billion pairs of the chemical bases adenine, cytosine, guanine, and thymine. Every gene specifies the manufacture of a specific protein that functions either to build body cells or to regulate the expression of other genes, and a huge proportion of genes are expressed in the central nervous system, where they affect brain development and behaviour. Rapid advances are taking place in our understanding of genetics. DNA molecules can now be cut into pieces, recombined with pieces of DNA from other sources, and inserted into host organisms, where they reproduce themselves exactly like ordinary DNA, and this is called genetic engineering. Behaviour genetics, which is concerned with the way hereditary and environmental factors interact in

determining behaviour, uses techniques such as family studies in which the behaviour of people of varying degrees of genetic relatedness is compared, twin studies in which behavioural similarities in identical twins (who share identical sets of genes) and non-identical twins (who share half their genes in common) are compared, and adoption studies in which individuals raised apart from their biological parents are examined for similarities with their adoptive and their biological parents.

Comparative psychology focuses on the similarities and differences between the behaviour of different animals. Investigations of the evolution of behaviour were greatly stimulated in the 1970s and 1980s by the growth of sociobiology, regarded by some as the most important advance in evolutionary theory since Darwin. According to the standard theory of evolution by natural selection, the frequency of a gene in a population increases if it increases the Darwinian fitness – the chances of survival and reproduction – of the organisms that possess it. But certain forms of behaviour that reduce the individual's chances of survival, such as the warning signals that birds give when they spot predators, appeared to contradict the theory until sociobiologists showed that natural selection operates on genes rather than individual organisms and that an organism must sometimes compromise its chances of individual survival in order to maximize the number of copies of its genes that it passes on.

The basic structural and functional units of the nervous system are cells called neurons. A neuron is a nerve cell specialized to transmit nerve impulses. It typically consists of a cell body together with branch-like dendrites that receive signals from other neurons, most neurons being involved in 1000 to 10,000 points of contact with other neurons, and an axon ranging in length from 3 micrometres to more than a metre that transmits signals away from the cell body to one or more other neurons or to a muscle or a gland. Neural transmission is an electrochemical process that is well understood. The nervous system is made up of afferent (sensory), efferent (motor), and internuncial (associative) neurons. It consists of the central nervous system – the brain and spinal cord – and the peripheral nervous system, which includes the somatic (sensory and motor) and the autonomic nervous systems. The autonomic nervous system is the largely self-regulating division of the nervous system that controls the involuntary and vegetative cardiovascular, digestive, reproductive, and respiratory functions of the body. It is subdivided into the sympathetic nervous system and the parasympathetic nervous system. The sympathetic nervous system consists of nerves originating from the spinal cord and supplying muscles and glands, and it is concerned with general activation and mobilizing the body's fight or flight reaction to stress or perceived danger. The parasympathetic nervous system acts in opposition to and with more specificity than the sympathetic nervous system and its main function is to conserve metabolic energy.

The brain is a far more complex mechanism than most people realize. It weighs only about 1440 grams but contains over ten thousand million neurons, most of which make thousands of connections with other neurons. It is far more complicated than the largest supercomputer, but the functions of some of its parts are gradually being mapped, at least in outline. Modern techniques of brain imaging, especially magnetic resonance imaging or MRI and positron emission tomography or PET scans, have led to rapid advances in our understanding of brain function. MRI is a non-invasive method of brain imaging that involves recording the responses of different kinds of molecules in a magnetic field to radio waves or other forms of energy. When it is used to provide a dynamic picture of oxygen metabolism in different parts of the brain during specific mental activities it is called functional MRI or fMRI. A PET scan is another non-invasive technique of brain imaging that monitors the blood flow in different regions of the brain by recording the emission of gamma rays when radioactively labelled glucose introduced into the bloodstream is metabolized by neurons as they are activated. The radioactive atoms emit subatomic particles called positrons (positive electrons), which collide with their negatively charged counterparts, namely electrons. The two particles annihilate each other and emit two gamma rays radiating in opposite directions that can be recorded by a ring of detectors round the person's head and traced back to their point of origin. These and other methods of brain imaging are leading to rapid advances in our understanding of brain processes.

Physiological psychology is the branch of psychology devoted to the relations between physiological and psychological processes and events. Neuropsychology is the study of the effects of disorders of the nervous system on behaviour and mental experience. Damage to specific areas of the cerebral hemispheres, the most complex and evolutionarily recent areas of the brain, leads to predictable disruptions of memory, perception, language, or motor co-ordination, and

diffuse cerebral damage degrades the ability to reason. Language and mathematical abilities are located in the left cerebral hemisphere in nearly all right-handed people and in about 70 per cent of left-handed people, whereas spatial and pattern recognition abilities are usually located in the right hemisphere. A vast amount of research has been devoted to studying electrical brain-wave activity through electroencephalogram (EEG) recordings from electrodes attached to people's scalps.

The endocrine system is the network of ductless glands that secrete hormones directly into the bloodstream, where they come into contact with specific receptors on target cells elsewhere in the body. The endocrine system functions as an extensive signalling system within the body, alongside the nervous system. Like the nervous system, it conveys messages from one part of the body to another, but whereas the nervous system sends its messages through nerve impulses, the endocrine system communicates via chemical hormones in the bloodstream. It is importantly implicated in emotional responses such as fear.

States of consciousness, including sleep and dreaming, have been studied partly through EEG recordings, and some details of this research were described in the answers to Questions 1 and 2 of the quiz. Research into the psychological effects of drugs, an area of investigation that is often called psychopharmacology, focuses on the following types of drugs, among others: depressant drugs such as alcohol, barbiturates, and benzodiazepines that slow the activity of the central nervous system; stimulants such as amphetamines, caffeine, and cocaine, that accelerate the activity of the central nervous system; narcotics such as morphine, methadone, and heroin that produce drowsiness, torpor, numbness, and loss of consciousness and are generally addictive; hallucinogens such as lysergic acid diethylamide (LSD), psilocybin, and dimethyltryptamine (DMT) that induce hallucinations or radically alter perception; and recreational drugs such as cannabis and ecstasy that induce euphoria.

2 *Sensation and perception*   (Questions 3, 5, 6, 7, 8, 9, 10, and 11 of the quiz) This is by far the oldest category of psychological research, and it is also one of the most successful. Sensation is conventionally differentiated from perception, although the distinction is philosophically and scientifically dubious. Sensation is the subjective experience or feeling that results from stimulation of a sense organ, and perception is the sensory experience interpreted with reference to its presumed external stimulus object or event after information processing and interpretation of the sensory information have taken place. This distinction was first made in the eighteenth century, but we now know that a great deal of processing of visual information (for example) takes place in the retina of the eye, and the notion of a pure sensation without any information processing is debatable at best. This category includes such topics as vision, shape perception, colour perception, movement perception, depth perception, hearing, sound localization, the chemical senses, the skin and body senses, psychophysics, and perceptual illusions.

Vision is the most thoroughly researched modality of sensation. The lens of the eye focuses light on to specialized cells in the retina called rods and cones that convert the light energy into electrical nerve impulses. Rods are brightness receptors. Cones, which are less numerous and much less sensitive, come in three varieties and are colour receptors. Visual signals are analysed in parallel by three separate processing systems. One system processes information about colour, and some of the details were discussed in the answer to Question 11 of the quiz. A second system processes information about static shape, and a third deals with movement and stereoscopic depth. The shape system and the movement and depth system are both colour-blind. It is difficult to see shape and impossible to see depth in images made up of different colours of equal brightness, and the movement of a coloured object is invisible when viewed against a differently coloured background of equal brightness – the object is seen in one position and then in another without appearing to have moved. The visual cortex contains some highly specialized cells that respond to specific features of shape and movement, including edges, lines moving in particular directions, bars oriented at particular angles, and so on, and these cells fire only when specific patterns of signals are received from the retinal images. The basic principles of depth perception through stereopsis were discussed in the answer to Question 3 of the quiz.

Hearing is the second most thoroughly researched mode of sensation. Sound waves cause the ear drum to vibrate, and the vibration is transmitted via three tiny bones in the middle ear to a coiled tube in the inner ear called the cochlea (from the Greek word for snail). The cochlea is filled with fluid and contains a flexible membrane called the basilar membrane. Because the cochlea tapers from one end to the other, the part of the basilar membrane that vibrates the most depends on the frequency of the sound. Resting on the basilar membrane are pointed structures called hair cells with auditory nerve cells connected to their bases. Vibrations of the basilar membrane cause the hair cells to bend back and forth, and this triggers nerve impulses to the brain. The pitch of the sound that is heard depends on which part of the basilar membrane vibrates the most and which nerve cells are therefore excited. The volume of the sound depends on the strength of vibration of the basilar membrane, which is translated into the rate at which the nerve cells fire.

The sensitivity of the ear is almost beyond belief. According to the Hungarian-born United States physicist Georg von Békésy, who earned a Nobel prize for his work on hearing in 1961, the weakest signal that can be heard moves the ear drum across a distance equivalent to one four-millionth of the diameter of a fine silk thread. Experiments have shown that hair cells in the inner ear begin to trigger nerve impulses when their tips move one ten-thousandth of a millimetre. Furthermore, the auditory system also has an ability to measure astonishingly small time differences between sounds reaching the two ears. This is necessary for sound localization, which was fully explained in the answer to Question 6 of the quiz.

The chemical senses, namely taste and smell, have received less attention from researchers, but the fundamental principles of their functioning are understood. Taste sensations occur when sapid (tasteable) substances that are dissolved in water or capable of being dissolved in saliva stimulate approximately 9000 taste buds located principally on the tongue but also in the soft palate, throat, pharynx and insides of the cheeks. The primary tastes are believed to be sweet, sour, salty, and bitter, and other tastes arise from combinations of these. Smells are experienced when molecules of aromatic substances are drawn into the upper nasal cavity and bind to cells that are specialized for specific kinds of odours and that respond by generating nerve impulses and transmitting them to the brain. The type or types of activated neurons indicate the quality of the odour and the number of activated neurons determine its intensity. The primary odours are believed to be fragrant (like lavender or rose petals), ethereal (like ether or cleaning fluid), resinous (like resin or turpentine), spicy (like cinnamon or nutmeg), putrid (like faeces or rotten eggs), and burnt (like tar oil).

A great deal is also known about the skin and body senses, including touch, kinaesthesis (sensations originating in the muscles, tendons, and joints), and the vestibular sense (the sense of orientation and balance originating in the inner ear). See the answers to Questions 7 and 8 of the quiz for details of psychophysics, and Questions 6, 9, and 10 for discussions of some interesting perceptual illusions.

3 *Cognition* (Questions 4, 10, 12, and 13 of the quiz) Roughly speaking, cognition (from Latin *cognoscere*, to apprehend) is information processing. This category includes memory, attention, imagery, language, thinking and problem solving, cognitive neuropsychology, and artificial intelligence. It usually excludes perception, although the line between perception and cognition is very blurred.

Memory is the process of encoding, storing, and retrieving information. It can be divided into three types called sensory, short-term, and long-term memory. Sensory memory, which is essential for normal vision and hearing, allows images to be stored for about half a second and sounds for up to 2 seconds. When we watch television, what appears on the screen is thirty separate still pictures per second, but what we see is a single moving image. For this to happen, we must be able to remember each still picture at least until the next one appears. Without sensory memory it would be impossible to understand a single spoken word, because by the end of the word we would have forgotten its beginning. Short-term memory is capable of holding a limited amount of information for brief periods, up to a few seconds, although it can be renewed repeatedly by being rehearsed. For example, when we need to remember a telephone number while searching for a pen or pencil with which to write it down, we often hold the information in short-term memory by repeating it under our breath or out loud every second or two, and sensory memory keeps the information alive during the gaps. The short-term memory store, sometimes called working memory, can hold only about seven digits or other items of information at a time. Without short-term memory, language would be incomprehensible, because to understand a sentence a listener or reader has to remember its beginning at least until its end.

Long-term memory is used for storing the meanings of words, the names of people, useful and useless facts, personal experiences, and other items of information that are preserved for extended periods of time. It also includes a type of knowledge called procedural knowledge regarding how to carry out sequences of operations, often without conscious awareness or verbal representation. The long-term memory store is large enough to hold far more information than anyone could encode in a single lifetime. Items of information in short-term memory that are repeated often enough are eventually transferred to the long-term store automatically. Some elementary findings of experimental research into long-term memory were discussed in the answer to Question 13 of the quiz.

Research into attention is motivated by the fact that people are simultaneously bombarded by sensory information of many different kinds but are able to think consciously and rationally about only one thing at a time. In 1957 the British psychologist Donald Broadbent proposed a filter theory, according to which there exists a central processing mechanism with a limited capacity that can select only one sensory input channel at a time and can switch between input channels no more than about twice per second, information in an unattended channel being held in short-term memory for a few seconds. While the rejected information is being held in short-term memory the filter, acting like a uniselector switch, allows the chosen information to enter the higher processing centres of the brain. Evidence for the theory was provided by experiments in which pairs of digits were presented simultaneously to both ears at a rate of up to two per second, and listeners invariably recalled them ear by ear rather than pair by pair, evidently switching attention from one ear to the other. Cognitive psychologists now believe that there are several dedicated processors operating in parallel, and that attention can be switched from sensory input to information output or action. In addition to pure research, a great deal of applied research has been done on attention. Eye movements of pilots, radar operators, and others have been recorded as a basis for deriving equations describing the distribution of attention in dynamic environments, and operator error can be reduced by designing instrument layouts that match the attentional demands of the task and the capacities of the operator.

Research into imagery is concerned with mental images formed by imagination and memory. The founding father of experimental psychology Wilhelm Wundt (1832–1920) believed that images are one of the three basic elements of consciousness, together with sensations and feelings. Psychologists investigate not only visual images but also images from the other senses, such as hearing, taste, smell, and touch. For most people, images are indistinct and fleeting, but some researchers claim that a significant minority of children and a much smaller proportion of adults are capable of eidetic imagery, in which visual images appear extremely clear and vivid, like ordinary perceptions. Imagery underlies several of the most effective mnemonic devices that can be used to memorize words, numbers, or other items, and it plays a key role in certain techniques of cognitive behaviour therapy.

The psychology of language, sometimes called psycholinguistics, includes the acquisition of language, the psychology of reading, the relationship between language and thought, psychological aspects of bilingualism, and several other sub-topics. Psychological investigations of language have been strongly influenced by a continuing debate over the ideas of the United States linguist Noam Chomsky, first published in the late 1950s. Chomsky argued that the rapidity and accuracy with which children learn to speak suggests that they are born with an innate knowledge of at least some universal structural principles of language.

Thinking and problem-solving depend on forms of reasoning that may or may not be strictly logical. Deductive reasoning is the derivation of conclusions from premises, and inductive reasoning is the establishment of generalizations from particular instances. The criterion for correct deductive reasoning is logical validity, but there is no criterion for inductive reasoning, although inductive reasoning is believed by some psychologists to play a part in scientific thinking, intuitive statistical judgements, and social inferences such as stereotypes of racial groups. One of the most influential developments in the psychology of thinking has been the idea of heuristics and biases introduced by the Israeli psychologists Amos Tversky and Daniel Kahneman in the 1970s. A heuristic is a rough-and-ready procedure or rule of thumb for making a decision, forming a judgement, or solving a problem without the application of an exhaustive calculation or examination of all available options, and hence without any guarantee of obtaining the right or optimal answer. One of the rules of thumb that is often used in everyday inductive reasoning is called the availability heuristic. This is a heuristic through which the frequency or probability of an event is judged by the number of instances of it that can be brought to mind. It can generate biased or incorrect judgements, as when people are asked whether the English language contains more words beginning with the letter k or more with k as the third letter. Most people find it easier to think of instances words beginning with k and therefore conclude that there are more words beginning with k, but in fact a typical long text contains twice as many words with k as the third letter. For the same reason, most people vastly overestimate the relative frequency of violent crimes and underestimate the relative frequency of non-violent crimes, because violent crimes are more often reported in the press and talked about, and as a result most people can think of more instances of them.

Cognitive neuropsychology is a topic that occupies the interface between cognitive psychology and neuropsychology. It is concerned with normal and impaired functioning in brain-damaged patients. For example, the validity of certain theories of reading and writing can be tested by studying the pattern of errors made by a brain-damaged patient and comparing it with the patterns of errors made by other patients. It turns out that people with certain forms of damage can read only by translating each letter into its corresponding sound, and they have great difficulty reading words with irregular spelling such as *yacht*. On the other hand, people with other forms of damage cannot translate letters into sounds and are able to read only by whole word recognition, as a consequence of which they have great difficulty reading simple non-words such as *varg*. This shows that at least two separate mechanisms are involved in reading.

Artificial intelligence (AI) is the science of designing machines to do things that are normally done by minds, such as playing chess, thinking logically, writing poetry, composing music, and analysing chemical substances. The most important applications of AI are to forms of intelligence that do not require (or even allow) conscious control, such as vision and language. The emphasis in AI is on software rather than hardware, and the focus of interest is on information processing. Some AI programs are designed to simulate human mental processes or brain physiology. One of the most influential contributions to AI is the computational theory of vision developed in the late 1970s by the British psychologist David Courtenay Marr and deliberately modelled on the human visual system. This theory is intended to show how the pattern of light falling on the retina is transformed into a symbolic representation of the shapes, colours, and movements in the scene being looked at – a task that turned out to be vastly more complicated than anyone had imagined. AI models of language have met with little success, apart from the important negative achievement of drawing attention to the unsuspected computational complexity of this almost universal human ability. AI programs can interpret natural human speech only if the vocabulary, syntax, and domain of discourse are drastically restricted.

An important development in AI in the 1990s was the introduction of connectionist models based on parallel distributed processing. This area of research is devoted to designing intelligent systems, composed of groups of interconnected processing units, in which items of knowledge are represented not by single locations but by patterns over collections of units, and these patterns are adaptive inasmuch as they are capable of learning from experience. Connectionist models are believed to provide a more flexible, powerful, and realistic model of brain processes than the earlier serial processing models.

4 Learning and skills (Questions 5 and 14 of the quiz) This category is traditionally distinguished from memory (an aspect of cognition), although the dividing line is rather arbitrary. In psychology, learning is interpreted as any change in behaviour brought about by experience. All mental and behavioural characteristics that are not wholly inborn are learnt in this sense. Most learning takes place without formal instruction or conscious effort on the part of the learner. Throughout our lives, we acquire political and religious beliefs and attitudes, personal habits, a large number of skills including the ability to speak and understand language, and a considerable general knowledge, for the most part without even realizing that we are engaged in learning processes. The basic principles of learning are similar in human and non-human species, and much of the research in this area is carried out on rats, pigeons, dogs, chimpanzees, and other animals. This category includes such topics as classical conditioning, instrumental or operant conditioning, learned helplessness, and skills.

Classical conditioning was discovered around the turn of the century by the Russian physiologist Ivan Petrovich Pavlov (1849–1936). Pavlov was studying salivation in dogs as part of his research into digestion, which earned him the first Nobel prize ever given to a physiologist or to a Russian. He devised an apparatus that enabled him to collect and measure the dogs' salivary responses to various kinds of food, and he soon noticed that the dogs began to salivate before the food was presented, when they heard the footsteps of the approaching experimenter. He began studying this phenomenon, and found that if a stimulus that would not ordinarily cause salivation, such as the sound of a bell, is repeatedly presented just before a small amount of dried meat powder is squirted into the dog's mouth, then the sound of the bell on its own soon causes the dog to salivate. In the terminology of classical conditioning, if an unconditioned stimulus (one like food that unconditionally causes salivation) is repeatedly paired with a conditioned stimulus (an initially neutral stimulus such as the sound of a bell), then a conditioned response is eventually formed.

Classical conditioning is a relatively simple form of learning, but it underlies many complex patterns of behaviour. For example, animal experiments have shown that decreases in blood sugar level can be classically conditioned by pairing a conditioned stimulus such as a light or a sound with injections of insulin, a hormone that lowers blood sugar level. Once the conditioned response is well established, presentation of the previously neutral conditioned stimulus without the insulin injections can trigger a rapid fall in blood sugar sufficiently severe to throw the animal into a state of physiological shock. This research suggests that classical conditioning may underlie certain disorders such as asthma that are known to have psychosomatic components in the form of physical symptoms that are triggered or aggravated by external stimuli or emotional factors.

The process of instrumental conditioning, also called operant conditioning, was discovered in the 1930s by the United States psychologist Burrhus F. Skinner (1904–1990). It is more flexible and practically applicable than classical conditioning. Its fundamental properties were explained in the answer to Question 14 of the quiz.

Learned helplessness was discovered by the United States

psychologist Martin Seligman in the 1970s. Experimental dogs were strapped into harnesses to prevent them escaping and were given a series of painful electric shocks. The next day, they were placed in a situation in which they had to respond to a warning signal by jumping over a low barrier in order to avoid further shocks. Most of the dogs became apathetic and listless, and most failed to learn this simple avoidance response, but a control group of dogs that had not been exposed to the inescapable shocks on the previous day learned the avoidance response quickly and easily. Some of the dogs that showed learned helplessness, as Seligman called it, had to be forcibly pushed over the barrier hundreds of times before they acquired the avoidance response. Learned helplessness has been demonstrated in human subjects as well as animals. Seligman concluded that it reduces the motivation to solve problems, interferes with the ability to learn from experience, and produces depression. He suggested that human depression may be a form of learned helplessness. For example, a person who spends a long time in an emotionally damaging but inescapable family situation may become depressed and unable to take positive steps to improve matters when opportunities present themselves.

Skills are complex, organized patterns of behaviour acquired through experience, and research in this area draws heavily on the findings of research into learning. Some skills such as mathematical or chess-playing abilities are called cognitive skills because they depend mainly on information processing or intellectual activity. Cognitive skills are distinguished from perceptual skills such as radar monitoring, from perceptual-motor skills such as typing or juggling, and from social skills such as non-verbal communication. All skills improve with training, practice, feedback, and guidance, but the rate of improvement generally slows down as the skill improves, and there are often periods when it stops improving altogether or even deteriorates slightly before starting to improve again. The emerging area of sports psychology applies research into skills to the performance of competitors in all types of sports.

5 *Motivation and emotion* (Questions 12 and 19 of the quiz) Motivation refers to the psychological processes that energize or drive behaviour. Emotional states tend to have motivational effects and to involve many of the same brain structures as motivational processes, which is why the two are generally grouped together. This category includes hunger and thirst, sex, social motivation,

cognitive dissonance, cognition-arousal theory of emotion, expression of emotion, and emotion and memory.

Psychologists used to think that hunger is caused by sensory impulses from the stomach signalling that it is empty, but it is now known that feelings of hunger persist even if all nerves leading from the stomach to the brain are cut. Hunger is a complex motivational state, influenced by many external factors in addition to internal hunger pangs and stomach contractions. A small structure at the base of the brain called the hypothalamus is known to play an important part in the regulation of feeding, but hunger is not well understood, and the causes of eating disorders such as anorexia nervosa and bulimia nervosa are still largely unknown. Sensations of thirst are triggered by receptor cells in the hypothalamus that send nerve impulses to the brain when the amount of fluid in these cells falls, and by sensors in the veins and kidneys that transmit impulses to the brain when the amount of fluid *surrounding* the cells falls.

Sexual motivation and behaviour, although they have been extensively studied, are only partly understood. They are strongly influenced by biological factors such as sex hormones, and in animals an important role is played by pheromones – chemical substances that are secreted by an organism and that affect the behaviour or physiology of other members of the same species. Hormones also affect human sexual motivation, but psychological triggers are more important in human beings. The human sexual response cycle includes the following sequence of phases: an appetitive phase involving sexual desire, fantasy, and appetite for sexual activity; an arousal phase characterized by sexual excitement and accompanied in the male by tumescence and erection of the penis and in the female by lubrication and expansion of the vagina and swelling of the external genitalia; an orgasmic phase in which climax occurs and the male ejaculates; a resolution phase in which muscular relaxation, feelings of well-being, and detumescence of the male penis occur; and a refractory period characterized by a lack of sexual desire and an incapacity of males to achieve erection of the penis.

Social motivation includes such drives as the need for achievement, the need for affiliation, and several other needs that have been discovered. A considerable amount of research has been devoted to them since the pioneering work of the United States psychologists Henry A. Murray in the 1930s and David McClelland in the 1950s and 1960s. Cognitive dissonance is a form of motivation whose source is entirely cognitive. Its main properties were outlined in the answer to Question 12 of the quiz.

Research into emotion has been influenced by the cognition-arousal theory since the early 1960s, when it was proposed by the United States psychologist Stanley Schachter. According to the theory, an emotional state arises when a person who is physiologically aroused attributes the physical symptoms of arousal to a particular cause. Numerous experiments have confirmed that people who are given stimulant drugs experience emotions such as fear, anger, elation, or amusement if they are led to believe that the cause of their physical sensations is not the drug but something that they have seen or heard that is frightening, annoying, exciting, or funny respectively. But there is evidence to show that this theory does not fully explain emotional experiences.

Facial expressions of the primary emotions of happiness, sadness, disgust, surprise, anger, and fear are probably innate rather than learnt, because they appear soon after birth, even in blind infants, and have been found to be similar and mutually recognizable in all cultures that have been investigated. Emotions influence

facial expressions, of course, but there is also a reverse causal relation according to which facial expressions influence emotions. Experiments in which facial muscles have been directly manipulated by electrical stimulation, or indirectly manipulated by instructing subjects to pull faces, have shown that facial expressions influence emotions surprisingly strongly.

Research on memory has shown that information learnt in an emotional state is most easily remembered in a similar state. This is a special case of state-dependent learning – material learnt in a drunken state is best remembered in a later drunken state, and so on. It helps to explain why pleasant experiences are more likely to be remembered by a person who is happy, and unpleasant experiences by someone who is unhappy and is likely to become even more unhappy as a result. In addition, research has revealed that depression generally interferes with memory and learning.

6 *Individual differences and personality* (Question 15 of the quiz) This category includes intelligence and aptitudes, dynamic theories of personality, personality traits, multi-trait theories, and situationist theory.

Intelligence has been intensively investigated ever since the French psychologists Alfred Binet and Theodore Simon constructed the first standardized IQ test in 1905. IQ tests are supposed to measure general intelligence, but there is some controversy over whether such a thing even exists. Research has consistently shown that people who are good at some kinds of thinking are generally good at others, and that people who are bad at some tend to be bad at others. It is very difficult indeed to devise *any* intellectual problem that is not more easily solved by people with high IQs than those with low IQs. Some psychologists interpret this as evidence for the existence of a global, unitary factor of intelligence, but others are impressed by the equally undeniable fact that people differ in their strengths and weaknesses and prefer to think of mental ability in terms of separate, overlapping factors or aptitudes. In any event, techniques for measuring intelligence and aptitudes are highly developed. Some aspects of research into intelligence were discussed in the answer to Question 15 of the quiz.

Personality (from Latin *persona*, an actor's mask) is an ill-defined concept referring to the whole constellation of psychological characteristics that differentiate people from one another. Some personality theorists include intelligence in their definitions of personality but most (illogically) do not.

Dynamic theories of personality are those of the Viennese physician Sigmund Freud (1856–1939) and his followers, according to which personality is shaped by a person's characteristic manner of handling instinctual drives and the anxieties associated with them. The structure of personality, according to Freud, consists of three interacting systems. The id is an irrational and largely unconscious reservoir of biological instincts and primitive emotions; the ego is a rational system that develops out of the id as a child learns to delay gratification in the light of physical and social realities; and the superego is a system that evolves out of the conflict between the id and the ego and functions partly as a conscience. In the course of development, Freud believed, a person's instinctual drives are concentrated successively in different bodily zones (oral, anal, phallic, and genital), and satisfaction or frustration at different stages of development partly explains different adult personality types. A great deal of research has been devoted to testing predictions from Freud's theory.

Some personality researchers have concentrated on single personality traits. One example of a thoroughly researched personality trait is field dependence–independence. It was first identified in 1949 by the United States psychologist Herman A. Witkin using the rod-and-frame test, a test in which a person sits in a completely darkened room and attempts to adjust a luminous rod to a vertical position within a tilted luminous frame. Field dependent people are unduly influenced by the tilted frame, whereas field independent people are able to discount the frame and concentrate on internal gravitational cues in judging the upright. More convenient paper-and-pencil measures of field dependence were later developed. In general, research has shown that field independent people are good at logical thinking, tend to be attracted to occupations like engineering, architecture, science teaching, and experimental psychology, and are often regarded by others as ambitious, inconsiderate, and opportunistic. In sharp contrast, field dependent people excel at interpersonal relations, are generally considered to be friendly, popular, warm, and sensitive, and are best suited to careers such as social work, elementary school teaching, clinical psychology, and counselling psychology.

The aims of multi-trait theories of personality are to identify the entire constellation of underlying traits that constitute the structure of personality and to explain differences between people according to their locations on these dimensions. A statistical technique called factor analysis is used to analyse the correlations between huge numbers of traits in order to reduce them to a small number of underlying or fundamental dimensions. This is analogous to reducing the multitude of distinguishable shades of colour to the three dimensions of hue, saturation, and brightness that account for all the differences. One of the most influential and intensively researched of the multi-trait theories is that of the German-born British psychologist Hans Eysenck (1916–1997), first proposed in a primitive form in the 1940s. The three fundamental dimensions in this theory are extraversion (associated with traits such as sociability, friendliness, enjoyment of excitement, talkativeness, impulsiveness, cheerfulness, activity, and spontaneity), neuroticism (worrying, moodiness, tenseness, nervousness, and anxiety), and psychoticism (feelings of persecution, irrational thinking, liking for very strong physical sensations, inhumane cruelty, and lack of empathy). Eysenck believed that these three factors are biologically based and largely hereditary, and he suggested where they might be located in the nervous system. However, by the early 1990s accumulating research led to a general consensus among personality researchers that there are five fundamental dimensions of human personality. The so-called Big Five are extraversion, neuroticism, agreeableness, conscientiousness, and openness to experience or intellect (intelligence).

An important current controversy in the field of personality research, instigated by the United States psychologist Walter Mischel in 1968, is the debate about situationism. Mischel amassed an impressive array of evidence that seemed to cast doubt on the fundamental assumption of all personality theories, namely that people display more or less consistent patterns of behaviour across situations. He drew particular attention to the low correlations between personality test scores and behaviour in everyday situations, and he concluded that behaviour can be more reliably predicted from past behaviour than from personality test scores. This implies that behaviour is merely predictive of itself and that theories of personality are largely futile. This situationist critique of personality generated a considerable amount of debate and research, some of it seeming to contradict Mischel's arguments and evidence. Most authorities now adopt an interactionist position, according to which human behaviour is dependent partly on internal personality factors, partly on external situational factors, and partly on interactions between the two.

7 Developmental psychology (Questions 4 and 15 of the quiz) Developmental psychology is concerned with psychological phenomena of all kinds in infants (literally, people too young to speak, from Latin *infans*, speechless), children, adolescents, adults, and old people, and all the psychological changes that occur across the lifespan. This category, which cuts across the others, includes the development of perception, cognition, language, skills, and social relationships.

In human beings, the sense organs are now known to be fully functional from birth, but a great deal must be learnt before infants can perceive the outside world as adults do. For example, the ability to judge distance and depth on the basis of the disparity between the images recorded by the two eyes (stereopsis) does not develop until about 6 months of age.

A vast amount of research has been devoted to cognitive development, partly because of the influential work of the Swiss psychologist Jean Piaget (1896–1980), and one important aspect of this work was outlined in the answer to Question 4 of the quiz. Thought processes develop through a series of predictable stages. At first, infants fail to understand that objects temporarily hidden from sight continue to exist. Children below about 6½ or 7 years of age are usually unable to deal properly with relational concepts (such as more, bigger, or heavier) or to deal correctly with problems involving conservation of number, substance, mass, and volume. The ability to consider hypothetical ideas and to follow an abstract logical argument does not develop until early adolescence.

Language development has been intensively studied. A child usually utters its first meaningful words near the end of its first year, and by the age of 3 years most children have a vocabulary of more than a thousand words. During the course of language development in the second or third year a child's use of words usually manifests errors of overextension (as when a child understands the word *daddy* to denote all men, or *cat* to denote all animals), underextension (as when a child understands the word *cup* to denote only one particular cup, as if the word were a proper noun), and mismatch (as when a child calls a toy drum a car). Even in their earliest speech, children demonstrate a remarkable understanding of the rules of grammar, and they acquire internalized knowledge of grammar with remarkable speed on the basis of fragmentary and degenerate input data. This led the US linguist Noam Chomsky (born 1928) to propose the existence of an innate mechanism underlying language learning.

One of the most important language skills investigated by developmental psychologists is reading. In logographic systems of writing such as Chinese, a child has to learn the relationship between each logogram and the word or phrase that it represents. In alphabetic systems such as English there is an extra step in the learning process: the child must learn to translate the written words into their sound equivalents before matching them with their appropriate concepts. The operations involved in learning to read therefore depend on the orthographic form of the text that is to be read. A significant amount of research has gone into children's reading and writing skills, and also into their drawing skills. Social development begins with the establishment of infant–mother attachment at about 6 months. In late infancy and early childhood, play serves as a method of practising and developing various skills, including social skills. Gender identity develops in a manner that is not yet fully understood but is the focus of a great deal of research. By 3 years of age, children are usually acutely conscious of gender, although they tend to confuse gender differences with the clothing and hairstyles typically associated with them. Play involving social pretence has been shown to be especially important in social development. When children play together, the groundwork of moral development is laid through experience of learning to obey rules. A great deal of research has focused on moral development and on the effects of various factors on the development of antisocial behaviour. For example, the effects of television violence have been extensively investigated.

8 *Social psychology* (Questions 12, 16, 18, 19, and 20 of the quiz) This category includes attitudes, conformity and obedience to authority, interpersonal attraction, attribution processes, group processes, helping behaviour, and non-verbal communication.

Attitudes are the favourable or unfavourable feelings, thoughts, and behavioural dispositions that people have towards other people, objects, and abstract ideas. Sophisticated techniques have been developed for measuring attitudes reliably and validly. An enormous amount of detailed experimental research has been devoted to attitude change and persuasion. The persuasive influence of a message is now known to depend on certain well-documented characteristics of the source, message, recipient, and channel of communication (face-to-face communication, films, television, radio, Internet, or the printed word). Attitude change often occurs for reasons of self-justification, and an example of this phenomenon was discussed in the answer to Question 12 of the quiz.

Research into conformity has examined the surprisingly powerful influence of group pressure on the behaviour, attitudes, and perceptions of individuals. Experiments on obedience to authority have focused on the related phenomenon of compliance with direct orders or instructions, a line of investigation that began in the mid-1960s with the discovery by the United States psychologist Stanley Milgram that a majority of ordinary people will deliver what they believe to be extremely painful and apparently lethal electric shocks to an innocent victim if merely ordered to do so by an authority figure.

Interpersonal attraction is another popular area of research in social psychology. Many of the factors influencing people's likes and dislikes for other people have been pinpointed, although some aspects of this process remain mysterious. One rather obvious factor that has been confirmed in laboratory and field studies is similarity – other things being equal, people tend to like those who share their attitudes and values. Studies of the development, maintenance, and breakdown of long-term relationships have revealed many of the unwritten rules that people expect to be followed in dating relationships, marriages, and other long-lasting social relationships.

Attribution processes are the ways in which people ascribe causes to their own behaviour and the behaviour of others. Research in this area attempts to identify and explain the unarticulated common-sense psychology of ordinary people. For example, it has been established that we tend to attribute another person's behaviour to internal, personal motives rather than external causes if the behaviour seems different from how other people would behave in the same situation but characteristic of that person's behaviour in similar and dissimilar situations in the past. If the behaviour seems similar to that of others in the same situation but uncharacteristic of that person's past behaviour in similar and different situations, then we are likely to attribute it to external causes. It has also been established that in most circumstances of everyday life people tend to attribute their own behaviour to external, situational causes and the behaviour of others to internal, personal causes, but this tendency can be overridden by a self-serving bias which leads people to attribute their own successes to internal, personal factors and their failures to external causes.

Group processes are, of course, of central interest to social psychologists. Many aspects of groups processes, including cooperation and competition, leadership emergence, and group decision making, have been studied. One important line of research into group decision making has examined the tendency of group decisions to be more extreme than individual decisions, and the main ideas and research findings were summarized in the answer to Question 18 of the quiz. Another important social psychological phenomenon, group inhibition of helping behaviour, was discussed in the answer to Question 20 of the quiz. Non-verbal communication has been intensively researched since video recording apparatus became widely available in the 1960s. Research has concentrated mainly on non-verbal aspects of speech (stress, intonation, loudness, and so on), facial expression, gaze and eye contact, gestures and other bodily communicative movements, touching and personal space, and inconsistencies that sometimes occur between a verbal message and the non-verbal body language that accompanies it, notably when people are lying. Interesting differences between cultures have been found in this area of research, some aspects of which will be outlined in chapter 4.

9 Abnormal psychology (Questions 15, 16, and 17 of the quiz) This category of psychology is devoted to the nature, aetiology (causes), diagnosis, treatment, and prevention of mental disorders. It underpins the profession of clinical psychology, which will be discussed in chapter 6. The classes of mental disorders in the internationally recognized *Diagnostic and Statistical Manual of Mental Disorders (DSM-IV)* issued by the American Psychiatric Association include the following, among others: disorders usually first diagnosed in infancy, childhood, or adolescence; schizophrenia and other psychotic disorders; mood disorders; anxiety disorders; factitious disorders; dissociative disorders; sexual and gender identity disorders; eating disorders; and personality disorders.

One of the disorders usually first evident in infancy, childhood, or adolescence is mental retardation, characterized by arrested or incomplete mental development, leading to significantly below-average intellectual functioning. It is accompanied by deficits in adaptive functioning in such areas as interpersonal communication, self-care, home living, social skills, use of public amenities, self-direction, scholastic or academic performance, work, leisure, health, or safety. Attention-deficit/hyperactivity disorder is another disorder in this class, affecting between 2 and 10 per cent of school-age children worldwide. It is at least three times as common in boys as in girls and is characterized by persistent inattention, hyperactivity, or impulsivity, causing problems at school or work and in the home. Also in this class is autistic disorder, which was discussed in the answer to Question 16 of the quiz.

Schizophrenia is a major mental disorder characterized by signs and symptoms such as delusions (false beliefs), hallucinations (false perceptions, such as hearing voices or seeing things that are not actually present), disorganized speech and behaviour, emotional flattening, and marked deterioration in work, social relations, or self-care. People with schizophrenia often show inappropriate emotional responses, are unable to experience pleasure or interest in formerly pleasurable activities, experience disagreeable or unpleasant moods, and lack the capacity to understand the abnormal or pathological nature of their condition. They sometimes experience feelings of emotional detachment or estrangement from themselves, as if they were acting in a play or observing their physical and mental activities from without, and they occasionally experience the external world as unreal, strange, or alien, as if it were a stage on which people were acting. People with paranoid schizophrenia experience delusions or hallucinations of being persecuted or harassed. Closely related to schizophrenia is delusional disorder, also called paranoia, characterized by delusions of being deceived by a sexual partner, loved from afar, persecuted or harassed, or having a physical abnormality. People with delusions of grandeur are also sometimes considered to have this disorder, one theory of which will be discussed in chapter 4.

One of the most serious mood disorders is major depressive disorder, characterized by episodes of depressed mood, markedly diminished interest or pleasure in almost all activities, loss of appetite or marked increase in appetite leading to significant weight loss or gain, and insomnia or excessive sleepiness. Other signs and symptoms of major depressive disorder include agitation manifested by such behaviour as hand-wringing, a general slowing of bodily movements including eye blinking and speech, fatigue or loss of energy, feelings of worthlessness or excessive or inappropriate guilt, indecisiveness or diminished ability to think or concentrate, and recurrent thoughts of death or suicide. Up to 15 per cent of people with major depressive disorder kill themselves each year. Bipolar disorders, which used to be called manic–depressive disorders, are characterized by manic episodes or mixed episodes and usually, but not necessarily, also major depressive episodes. Manic episodes are episodes of continuously elevated, expansive, or irritable mood, sufficiently severe to cause marked impairment in social or occupational functioning or to require hospitalization, during which the person may show inflated self-esteem or grandiose ideas or actions, decreased need for sleep, increased talkativeness, flight of ideas, distractibility and risky pleasure-seeking activities such as spree shopping, sexual indiscretions, or imprudent financial investments. Mixed episodes are mood episodes with both manic and depressive characteristics.

Anxiety disorders include a variety of conditions in which anxiety features prominently. One of the most common is agoraphobia, characterized by fear of leaving home, being in a crowd, visiting public places such as shopping areas, travelling alone in buses, trains, or aircraft, or being in other situations from which escape might be awkward or where a panic attack would be difficult to handle. Another common anxiety disorder is generalized anxiety disorder, in which there is excessive and largely uncontrollable anxiety not focused on any specific circumstances but related to everyday events or activities such as problems at work or school, with symptoms of restlessness, tiredness, difficulty concentrating, irritability, muscle tension, or sleep disturbance. A third common anxiety disorder is obsessive–compulsive disorder, characterized by recurrent and persistent thoughts, impulses, or ideas that cause significant distress and are experienced as intrusive or inappropriate, or repetitive patterns of behaviour such as hand-washing, tidying, checking, praying, counting, or reciting words or phrases silently that a person feels compelled to perform, following strict rules or rituals, with the aim of relieving anxiety or avoiding some dreaded outcome. Post-trauma stress disorder is an anxiety disorder arising as a delayed response to a traumatic experience and resulting in intense fear, helplessness, or horror, and persistent re-experiencing of the trauma through distressing recollections, recurrent dreams, sensations of reliving the experience, hallucinations, or flashback experiences. Associated symptoms may include intense distress in response to anything reminiscent of the traumatic event, a numbing of emotions, insomnia, irritability, and difficulty concentrating.

Factitious disorder, also called Munchausen syndrome after Baron Münchhausen, a teller of tall stories in the fiction of the German novelist Rudolf Erich Raspe, involves a persistent pattern of feigned symptoms and/or self-inflicted injuries designed to simulate a physical disorder, without any economic or other external incentive for the behaviour (such as escaping military service or obtaining health insurance payouts), the motive being to receive medical treatment, to gain admission to hospital, or to assume the sick role. People with this condition often undergo multiple unnecessary surgical operations before their true condition is discovered. In the related condition called factitious disorder by proxy or Munchausen by proxy syndrome, a person intentionally feigns medical signs or symptoms in a child or person being cared for with the aim of procuring medical treatment for that person or assuming a sick role by proxy. Strictly speaking, it is not a psychological disorder but a form of physical or psychological abuse of children or others being cared for.

Dissociative disorders involve partial or total disconnection between memories of the past, awareness of identity and of immediate sensations, and control of bodily movements. They often result from traumatic experiences, intolerable problems, or disturbed relationships. Included in this class are conditions such as dissociative amnesia (loss of memory, usually for important recent events associated with serious problems, stress, or unexpected bereavement), dissociative fugue (sudden unexpected travel away from home, with amnesia for some or all of the past, confusion about personal identity, and occasionally the assumption of a new identity), and dissociative identity disorder, also called multiple personality disorder (two or more separate personalities, each with its own memories and patterns of behaviour, alternately taking control of behaviour).

Among the most common sexual disorders are the sexual dysfunctions. In female and male orgasmic disorder there is a persistent or recurrent delay or absence of orgasm following the excitement phase of the sexual response cycle. More common among men is male erectile disorder, a sexual dysfunction characterized by persistent or recurrent inability to attain or maintain an adequate erection of the penis until completion of sexual activity, believed to afflict approximately 10 per cent of adult males, and premature ejaculation, a condition in which orgasm and ejaculation are triggered by minimal sexual stimulation and occur before they are wanted, usually before or around the time of penetration, making sexual intercourse difficult or impossible. Also included in this class are the paraphilias, a large group of sexual disorders involving recurrent sexually arousing fantasies, sexual urges, or behaviour that are regarded as disorders if they cause clinically significant distress or impairment in social, occupational, or other important areas of functioning. Among the most common paraphilias are sexual masochism (involving submission to pain, humiliation, bondage, or some other form of physical or psychological suffering), sexual sadism (involving the subjection of another person to pain, humiliation, bondage, or some other form of physical or psychological suffering), and paedophilia (fantasies, urges, or behaviour involving sexual activity with prepubescent girls or boys). Gender identity disorder involves a strong and persistent identification with the opposite sex, coupled with discomfort with one's own sex or gender role, commonly manifested by cross-dressing or transvestism and occasionally leading people to seek sex-change operations.

The most prominent eating disorders are anorexia nervosa and bulimia nervosa. Anorexia nervosa, popularly but misleadingly called the slimmers' disease, occurs mostly in adolescent girls and young women who develop an intense fear of becoming fat that persists even when they are severely underweight. People with the disorder starve themselves and often show disturbances in body image, perceiving themselves to be fat even when they are emaciated. Bulimia nervosa is also far more common in women than men. It is characterized by recurrent episodes of binge eating, often carried out in secret, accompanied by a sense of loss of control, followed by feelings of shame and compensatory behaviour intended to prevent weight gain. The most common compensatory behaviours are self-induced vomiting, misuse of laxatives or diuretics, enemas, fasting, and excessive exercise. People with bulimia nervosa, like those with anorexia nervosa, attach undue emphasis to body shape and weight in their judgements of themselves, and the two disorders are closely related.

One of the most serious of the personality disorders is antisocial personality disorder. People with this disorder used to be called psychopaths or sociopaths. The disorder is characterized by a pervasive violation of the rights of others, beginning in childhood or early adolescence and continuing into adulthood. The signs and symptoms include failure to conform to social norms, leading in many cases to habitual law-breaking, repeated lying or swindling for pleasure or personal gain, impulsivity or failure to plan ahead, irritability and aggressiveness involving frequent assaults or fights, reckless disregard for the safety of self or others, failure to hold down jobs or to honour financial obligations, and lack of remorse for the mistreatment of others. A large proportion of serious crime is committed by people with this disorder. Another personality disorder is avoidant personality disorder, characterized by a pervasive pattern of social inhibition, feelings of inadequacy, and hypersensitivity to criticism, disapproval, or rejection. People with this disorder tend to avoid work involving significant interpersonal contact and are unwilling to associate with people unless they are confident of being liked. They are restrained in intimate relationships for fear of being shamed or ridiculed and are preoccupied with criticism or rejection, and reluctant to engage in activities carrying the risk of embarrassment.

10 *Research methods and statistics*   (not dealt with specifically in the quiz) This category includes qualitative and quantitative research methods, case studies, observational studies, survey methods, correlational studies, quasi-experiments, experimental design, and statistics. It is often taught to undergraduates through practical classes. It is discussed in detail in chapter 4.

11 *History of psychology*   (not dealt with specifically in the quiz) In this category are all topics in the history of psychology, from its earliest beginnings in ancient philosophy, through its modern philosophical and biological antecedents and older systems and theories, to contemporary research. An overview of the history of psychology is provided in chapter 5.

Further reading

Many good textbooks of psychology are available, and most of them cover the major areas of psychology and contain recommendations for further reading in specific areas. Among the most popular is *Hilgard's introduction to psychology* by R.L. Atkinson, R.C. Atkinson, E.E. Smith, D.J. Bem, and S. Nowlen-Hoeksema (12th ed., New York: Harcourt Brace, 1996). Another superb introductory text is Robert J. Sternberg's *In search of the human mind* (2nd ed., New York: Harcourt Brace, 1998).

In the United Kingdom Nicky Hayes's *Foundations of psychology: An introductory text* (2nd ed., Walton-on-Thames: Nelson, 1998) and Richard D. Gross's *Psychology: The science of mind and behaviour* (3rd ed., London: Hodder & Stoughton, 1996) are popular, and they are both highly recommendable.

A reference work rather than a textbook that contains authoritative entries on a wide range of psychological topics is *The Oxford companion to the mind*, edited by Richard L. Gregory (Oxford:

Oxford University Press, 1987), and the *Companion encyclopedia of psychology* edited by me, Andrew M. Colman (London: Routledge, 1994) contains chapters on all major areas of psychology, including the most important fields of applied psychology.

Chapter 4

Research methods and statistics

The starting-point of any research project is a question. The question may be purely factual, like some of the quiz questions in chapter 2, or practical, like the questions that concern applied psychologists (see chapter 6). It may arise from simple curiosity about everyday experience (for example, how often do we dream?), from a need to solve a practical problem (how can we cure an irrational fear of spiders?), or from a theory that generates prediction (does the sensation of visual brightness obey Weber's law?). Whatever its origin, if it is a question about the nature, functions, or phenomena of behaviour or mental experience and if it can be answered, in principle at least, by empirical methods, which means by systematic observation and objective evidence, then it is a psychological question. The goals of psychological research, or of any scientific research for that matter, are to describe, understand or explain, predict, and control the phenomena that are investigated. Research does not always seek to achieve all of these goals, and the goals are not all equally important; understanding or explanation is basic or fundamental and the others are subsidiary.

Before a psychological question can be subjected to research, it needs to be formulated as clearly as possible. After formulating the question, a competent researcher usually reviews the existing knowledge in specialist journals and books, and perhaps also on the Internet, to see whether it has been tackled before and whether research has been devoted to any closely related questions. The next step is hypothesis formulation, which amounts to making an informed guess about the answer to the question. Having formulated the hypothesis, the researcher is then in a position to design a method of investigation suitable for testing the hypothesis by checking predictions that flow from it.

In practice, research is often much more informal and haphazard than this. Questions are often formulated rather vaguely, hypotheses are sometimes implicit rather than explicit, and discoveries occasionally arise through serendipity rather than careful planning. Basic research (sometimes called theoretical research) is designed to test explicit hypotheses or theories, and it involves description, explanation, and prediction, but not control in the sense of modifying the phenomena that it studies. Exploratory research, which is sometimes used to make the first forays into unfamiliar territory when studying a new or poorly understood phenomenon, is usually largely descriptive, and what distinguishes it from other kinds of research is that it is not guided by any explicitly formulated hypotheses (it does not involve prediction), and it does not aim to solve practical problems (it does not involve control). Applied research is concerned with applications of psychology to practical problems of everyday life, and it therefore involves control in the sense of modifying the phenomena that it studies in addition to describing, explaining, and predicting them. The major applications of psychology outlined in chapter 6 are sustained largely by applied research.

The diversity of psychology's subject matter is reflected in the wide range of its research methods. These research methods all have the same fundamental goal of answering specific questions through disciplined investigations of objective evidence. But different research methods are best suited to different problems, and the particular questions under investigation sometimes constrain the choice of research methods. Although it would be misleading to suggest that some methods are intrinsically better than others, because different questions call for different methods, it is undeniable that the experimental method is the most powerful of all when it is applicable, because it can answer certain types of questions that the others cannot. The reasons for this will be explained in due course.

Qualitative research

The majority of published research in psychology is quantitative inasmuch as it relies on numerical data, but qualitative research became increasingly popular in certain areas of psychology during the 1990s. Qualitative research focuses on non-numerical data, which in practice usually means verbal data collected through interviews or records of naturally occurring speech or writing. One of the most important qualitative research methods is discourse analysis, an approach to understanding all forms of speech and written texts that views language as not merely describing and referring to reality but also constructing it. Some forms of discourse analysis are influenced by deconstruction, a method of textual analysis associated especially with the writings of the French philosopher and literary critic Jacques Derrida.

Especially in social psychology, qualitative research sometimes uses techniques of ethnomethodology, an approach to the study of human communication, introduced in 1967 by the United States sociologist Harold Garfinkel, that emphasizes common-sense language and interpretations of the world, and that makes considerable use of participant observation, a research methodology in which the investigator participates in the activities of a group while recording the behaviour of the other group members.

Another increasingly popular qualitative research technique is the use of focus groups, introduced in 1956 by the United States sociologist Robert K. Merton and widely used in market research since the 1960s to assess people's reactions to products, services, and advertisements. A focus group is a small group of people selected and assembled for research purposes, to participate in an organized discussion, under the guidance of a moderator, of an issue or topic of which they have personal experience. Proponents of focus groups believe that interaction between group members adds something important that is lacking in conventional interviews.

More radical qualitative methods include phenomenology, a philosophical method of enquiry founded in 1901 by the German philosopher Edmund Husserl that involves the detailed description of conscious experience while attempting to bracket (exclude) all preconceptions, interpretations, and explanations. Another radical qualitative method is the development of grounded theory, a technique of theory construction that reflects the interpretations of the research participants rather than those of the investigators. Both phenomenology and grounded theory depart fundamentally from the traditional empirical methods of psychology, and both are highly controversial.

Before discussing statistics, I shall review the most widely used experimental and non-experimental research methods, namely case studies, observational studies, survey methods, correlational studies, quasi-experiments, and controlled experiments. Case studies and observational studies often rely on techniques of qualitative research, whereas the other methods generally use quantitative research, but quantitative techniques can be used even in case studies and observational studies, and qualitative techniques can play a part in any research method, including a controlled experiment.

Case studies

A psychological case study is a detailed investigation of a single person, or occasionally a single organized group. Investigations of this type are extensively used in abnormal psychology, where they usually take the form of detailed descriptions of individuals with unusual or scientifically interesting psychological disorders or their responses to specific methods of treatment. They are less common in other areas of psychology, although they are occasionally used for studying individuals who have undergone unusual experiences that might have interesting psychological consequences. The detailed investigation of S.B. following his recovery from lifelong blindness, discussed in the answer to Question 5 of the quiz, is a typical case study of this kind. It shows how a case study can occasionally provide objective evidence and give a definite answer to a question of considerable scientific importance. The data reported in case studies are often collected by qualitative research methods, especially interviews, written records such as diaries and case notes, and direct observations of naturally occurring behaviour, but quantitative methods such as questionnaires and other psychometric tests are sometimes used.

Case studies are sometimes useful for formulating theories. An instructive example is the case study on the basis of which Sigmund Freud developed his theory of paranoia in 1911, and it is worth examining this example in detail. Paranoia, technically called delusional disorder nowadays, is a mental disorder characterized by delusions (false beliefs) of certain specific kinds. Freud was puzzled by the fact that paranoid delusions encountered in clinical practice are not entirely haphazard and unpredictable but tend to fall into the following four highly specific categories:

1   *Jealousy*: People with paranoia often have delusions that their sexual partners are being unfaithful.

2   *Erotomania*: Some people with paranoia have delusions of being loved by other people, often famous people or people of higher status in the workplace.

3   *Persecution*: People with paranoia very often have delusions that others are plotting to harm or kill them.

4   *Grandeur*: Many people with paranoia believe that they are gods, emperors, or famous or powerful people.

Freud therefore posed the following question. Why are paranoid delusions usually of these four types? What is special about these particular delusions? In a technically virtuosic case study based on the memoirs of Dr Schreber, a German magistrate who suffered from paranoid delusions for many years, Freud came to the surprising conclusion that an unconscious homosexual wish-fantasy lies at the heart of paranoia and explains the specific types of delusions that characterize it. The unconscious wish-fantasy of any man with paranoid delusions may be expressed in the following sentence: *I (a man) love him (a man)*.

Because homosexuality is socially taboo, a man with paranoia strives unconsciously to distort the wish-fantasy to avoid having to confront it consciously. There are four possible methods of distorting it into a more acceptable form. The first method is by changing the grammatical subject of the sentence through a defence mechanism that Freud called projection – attributing one's own unconscious impulses to other people. The distorted version is then *It is not I, but she (my sexual partner), who loves him*, and the man develops delusions that his sexual partner is being unfaithful with all the men towards whom he is unconsciously attracted. Second, a man with paranoia may distort the grammatical object of the sentence: *I don't love a man, because I love women*. In this form, the wish-fantasy is still unacceptable, at least to a Victorian married man, and it is therefore distorted further by projection into *Women love me*, and delusions of erotomania arise. Third, the verb of the sentence may be distorted by turning it into its opposite: *I do not love a man, I hate men*. But once again, because it is socially unacceptable to go around hating people for no good reason, it is distorted further by projection into *Men hate me*, and delusions of persecutions arise. At this point in his case study, Freud seems to have run out of methods of distorting the sentence, but he still has one class of delusions to explain. He delivers the *coup de grâce* by pointing out that there is, in fact, one more method. A man with paranoid delusions may deny the whole sentence: *I don't love a man, because I love no one.* But sexual energy cannot evaporate into thin air, according to Freud, so this statement is equivalent to *I love no one but myself*, and this accounts for delusions of grandeur. If the person with paranoia is female, then the whole chain of argument applies with all the gender terms reversed.

Freud's theory of paranoia or delusional disorder is intellectually dazzling and logically satisfying. Whether it is true or not is a different question altogether. Like most of Freud's theories, it is difficult to evaluate scientifically. At least four testable predictions can be inferred from it: (a) people with paranoia should show evidence of repressed homosexuality; (b) paranoia should not occur in practising homosexuals, because they do not have an *unconscious* homosexual wish-fantasy; (c) delusions of persecution in men with paranoia should involve only male persecutors; and (d) delusions of persecution in women with paranoia should involve only female persecutors. Clinical case studies have been carried out to test the theory, and most have confirmed its predictions, but the objectivity of their results has been questioned by critics, and the jury is still out.

Both case studies and experiments have been used to test the first and most fundamental assumption that people with paranoid delusions are repressed homosexuals. For example, one experiment tested the hypothesis that, if words with homosexual connotations are briefly flashed on to a screen, then people diagnosed with paranoia or delusional disorder should recognize the words more quickly than other people because, according to the theory, they are especially sensitive to this issue. Words with homosexual connotations such as *fairy* and *queer*, words with heterosexual connotations such as *caress* and *screw*, and non-sexual words were flashed on to a screen, and recognition times were measured. The hypothesis was confirmed: people with paranoia recognized the homosexual words (and only those words) significantly more quickly than people with other mental disorders and people without any mental disorder. These findings seem to support Freud's fundamental assumption, and it is not easy to see how else they could be explained, but on the other hand it could be argued that exactly the opposite hypothesis could have been formulated on the ground that repressed homosexuals should tend to *avoid* recognizing words with homosexual connotations. It is an acknowledged weakness of psychoanalytic theories that they often generate mutually contradictory predictions.

The aim of Freud's case study of Dr Schreber was nothing short of the construction of a new theory of paranoia or delusional disorder. Most case studies are more modest in their aims. But provided that it is reasonable to assume that what is true of the individual case applies equally to a larger class of people – a condition that is not always met – the findings of case studies can provide valuable insights into psychological processes.

Observational studies

Observational studies are widely used in certain areas of developmental and social psychology, and in ethology, an approach to the study of animal and human behaviour in natural habitats that was founded in the 1930s by the Austrian zoologist Konrad Lorenz. The answer to Question 19 of the quiz was based largely on the findings of observational studies of sexual practices and beliefs in various human societies. In contrast to case studies, which may involve interviews and psychometric tests, observational studies are non-interactive in so far as the investigator refrains as far as possible from interfering with or influencing the behaviour under observation. Observational studies tend to be less narrowly focused than most other research methods, they often rely on qualitative research techniques, and in most cases they are descriptive or exploratory in spirit, although they sometimes seek to provide explanations and predictions as well.

A typical area of research in social psychology in which observational studies are often used is non-verbal communication. One aspect of non-verbal communication that will suffice for illustrative purposes is the study of proxemics – the spatial features of human social interaction. Observational studies have uncovered surprisingly strict, though largely unconscious, rules and social conventions governing the use of personal space. They have shown that the optimal nose-to-nose distance for ordinary social interactions in the United States and northern Europe is 30 to 48 inches (76 to 122 centimetres). Even quite small deviations outside these limits in either direction (too close or too far) tend to produce visible signs of discomfort and efforts to re-establish conventional distances. Other cultures have proxemic conventions that are different but equally strict. Arab cultures, and also to a lesser extent Mediterranean cultures, prescribe much closer interpersonal distances for ordinary interactions, so that when an Arab talks to an

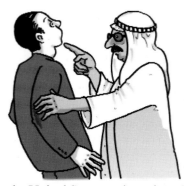

American (for example), the Arab may keep stepping forward while the American keeps retreating, and both may feel uncomfortable. Observational studies have revealed that cultures with proxemic rules prescribing close interpersonal distances usually allow much more body contact between relative strangers than the so-called non-contact cultures of the United States and northern Europe.

The effects of invasions of personal space have attracted specific attention from researchers. The narrowing of interpersonal distance usually communicates an attempt to increase the level of intimacy of an interaction. The appropriate distance for intimate conversations in non-contact cultures is about 6 to 18 inches (15 to 46 centimetres), and if both parties agree that the interaction is intimate they will feel comfortable at that distance and may even try to diminish it to zero if the relationship is highly intimate. But a party to the interaction who does not agree with this implied definition of the relationship usually tries to increase the distance or, failing that, to reduce the level of intimacy conveyed by other non-verbal signals such as eye-contact, facial expression, and vocal quality, in an attempt to compensate for the excessively close physical proximity. Intimacy-avoiding manœuvres like these have also been noted in observational studies of crowded lifts or elevators, underground trains, and similar social gatherings in which physical proximity is uncomfortably close for the level of intimacy of the situation.

The range of psychological phenomena that can be investigated through observational studies is limited, but where it is appropriate it can often yield illuminating insights. It has the advantage over other research methods of focusing on behaviour that is entirely natural. But the techniques of recording observations are often informal and unsystematic, and the findings of observational studies often raise questions about objectivity, because different observers may describe or interpret the same behaviour in quite different ways.

Survey methods

The aim of survey research in psychology is to investigate questions of psychological interest in specified sections of a population or in different populations. Investigations that focus on comparisons between different cultures are called cross-cultural surveys. Surveys that are confined to single populations usually examine differences between demographic groups defined by variables such as geographical location, ethnic identity, age, sex, social class, marital status, and education. The answer to Question 16 of the quiz was based on surveys of the distribution of schizophrenia, autistic disorder, and other mental disorders across the social class hierarchy in industrial societies. Survey research is usually purely descriptive, and it is used to answer questions about the prevalence and distribution of attitudes, opinions, beliefs, personality characteristics, mental disorders, and behaviour patterns. It raises special problems of research design and methodology, because a survey is reliable and valid only if the sample is representative and the respondents' replies are truthful.

The representativeness of a sample depends on the method of sampling that is used. A survey researcher needs to ensure that the individuals who are surveyed are truly representative of the population to which they belong. In small populations it is sometimes possible to carry out census surveys in which, by definition, every member of the population is investigated and therefore problems of sampling bias do not arise. This was the method used by Hollingshead and Redlich in their survey of psychiatric patients in New Haven, discussed in the answer to Question 16 of the quiz. But in most cases it is feasible to investigate only a small proportion of the population of interest, and this raises the problem of sampling bias.

In an ideal world, the sampling method of choice would be simple random sampling, in which the investigator selects individuals from the population strictly at random. This technique ensures that every member of the population has an equal chance of being included in the sample and that, provided the sample is reasonably large, it will contain roughly the right proportions of people in the various age, sex, social class, and other demographic categories relative to the parent population from which it is drawn, in other words that it will be truly representative, within a margin of error that can be calculated precisely using statistical methods. But simple random sampling is seldom used in practice because of the difficulty of compiling a list of all members of the population, called a sampling frame, from which a random selection can be made. Electoral registers are sometimes used as sampling frames, but they tend to omit certain sections of the population and they go out of date quite rapidly. In the United Kingdom, they are approximately 9 per cent inaccurate even when they are first published, and they deteriorate rapidly as people move about. Telephone directories are sometimes used as cheap and cheeky sampling frames, but in the United Kingdom approximately 10 per cent of people do not have telephones at home, and 25 per cent of people who do are ex-directory. Telephone directories produce biased samples with too few young people and poor people (the people without telephones) and too few women living alone (the most common ex-directory subscribers).

Various alternative methods of sampling have been developed. An excellent approximation to simple random sampling that is used by opinion polling organizations is random digit dialling. Within each telephone exchange (usually identified in the United Kingdom by the first four digits), the last few digits are dialled at random to contact each respondent. This is not simple random sampling because there is no sampling frame and because every member of the population does not have an equal chance of being included in the sample. Although it is much better than selecting numbers at random from telephone directories, because it includes ex-directory subscribers, it is slightly biased against younger, poorer people. Another popular technique is stratified random sampling, in which simple random sampling is applied separately to different sections of the population to ensure that all sections are represented in the right proportions and that (for example) young people and poor people are not underrepresented. It sometimes happens that no sampling frame of individual respondents exists but a sampling frame of *groups* of respondents can be found, and in these cases the technique of cluster sampling is available. For example, if a survey is required of all schoolchildren in the country, and there is no list of the schoolchildren from which a simple random sample can be drawn, then it may be possible to obtain a list of all schools in the country, to select schools (clusters) at random from it, and then to select children from each of the chosen schools by a random or non-random method. That would be an example of cluster sampling.

In practice, simple random sampling, stratified random sampling, cluster sampling, and other random sampling techniques are expensive, difficult, or unsatisfactory for other reasons. They seldom produce samples that are truly random or representative, because certain categories of people are more likely than others to refuse to participate or may slip through the net for other reasons. Often these methods are simply infeasible. To sidestep all the problems, a technique that is commonly used by psychological survey researchers, and also by opinion polling and market research organizations, is quota sampling. This involves selecting individuals in a hit-and-miss fashion, often by stopping people in the street or knocking more or less haphazardly on doors, until the sample contains predetermined quotas of people in various demographic categories such as age, sex, and social class reflecting the known proportions in the population at large. Survey researchers have found in practice that quota sampling is approximately as reliable as random sampling, and it is usually cheaper and easier to carry out.

But quota sampling is only as good as the data that are used to determine the relevant demographic proportions in the population. The most notorious failure of this technique occurred in a Gallup poll published just before the United States Presidential Election of 1948. The Gallup organization selected a quota sample of the United States electorate but used information about the relevant demographic proportions from the 1940 census. The industrial boom that had followed the Second World War in 1945, and the returning servicemen, had caused significant demographic changes in the population, and as a result Gallup's quota sample was badly biased. Gallup predicted a landslide victory for Dewey over Truman (by 49 to 44 per cent), and the result seemed so certain that the *Chicago Daily Tribune* even printed an early edition with the banner headline "DEWEY DEFEATS TRUMAN", but in the event Harry S. Truman won the 1948 election by a margin of 50 to 45 per cent.

Having selected a sample, the next task confronting a survey researcher is to extract the required data from the respondents. The reliability and validity of a survey depends on the accuracy and truthfulness of the respondents' replies. The most common sources of data are interviews and questionnaires, and such data are vulnerable to several subtle forms of bias. Tiny and seemingly insignificant variations in the phrasing of questions, or in the non-verbal signals conveyed by an interviewer, can have dramatic effects on the answers. Survey researchers have learnt through bitter experience that people's answers to certain kinds of questions cannot be taken at face value. For example, in a survey of attitudes towards organized religion, a person who is asked the apparently straightforward question *Are you in favour of organized religion?* may answer *Yes* for all sorts of reasons – because of a strongly held attitude in favour of organized religion; because of a weakly held attitude in favour of organized religion; because of a belief that an affirmative answer will convey a better impression to the interviewer than a negative answer; because of a tendency, called acquiescence response set, that causes some people to answer *Yes* to most questions irrespective of their content; because of a belief that the interviewer would prefer an affirmative answer; and so on.

A great deal is known about how people answer questions, and some of the problems of interviews can be overcome or reduced by the use of paper-and-pencil questionnaires. A properly constructed questionnaire is an objective measuring instrument whose validity has been checked, either by determining how successfully it discriminates between known criterion groups or by some other method. For example, to check the validity of a questionnaire to measure attitudes towards organized religion, criterion groups of regular church attenders and members of secular or humanist societies may be compared. Sophisticated techniques are available for constructing questionnaires that have high discriminating power and other desirable characteristics. Acquiescence response set can be taken care of simply by wording half the items in the questionnaire so that a *Yes* answer indicates a favourable attitude, like the question mentioned in the previous paragraph, and half the items so that a *Yes* answer indicates a negative attitude (for example, *Does organized religion do more harm than good?*). This is called counterbalancing, and it ensures that acquiescence response set will not bias the overall scores one way or the other.

In general, people's responses to survey questions are more truthful than one might imagine, but on sensitive issues such as sex, drugs, or criminal behaviour lies and half-truths can distort the results. For very sensitive issues, an ingenious technique called randomized response is sometimes used to reduce evasive response bias by ensuring respondent confidentiality. A randomizing device serves the purpose of concealing individual replies while preserving the group data that the survey researcher requires. For example, in a survey to estimate the proportion of people in a population who have had an HIV/AIDS test, a survey researcher might instruct the respondents to toss a coin without letting anyone else see which way it falls and then to answer *Yes* if *either* the coin falls heads *or* the answer to the question *Have you had an HIV/AIDS test?* is yes. It is impossible to determine from the survey replies which of the respondents have been HIV/AIDS tested, but the percentage who have been tested can be estimated from the data none the less. If no one in the population has been HIV/AIDS tested, then the proportion of *Yes* replies should be 50 per cent, with a margin of error that can be determined statistically. Suppose that 55 per cent reply *Yes*. Provided that the sample is large enough and the replies truthful, this means that approximately 10 per cent of the population must have had the HIV/AIDS test, and there is evidence that this technique does indeed tend to increase truthful responding.

Correlational studies

As the name implies, a correlational study is a research investigation in which the pattern of correlations between two or more variables is studied. A correlation is a measure of the degree of relationship between two variables indicating that high scores on one of the variables tend to go with high scores on the other or, in the case of negative correlation, that high scores on one tend to go with low scores on the other. The most commonly used index of correlation ranges from 1.00 for perfect positive correlation, through zero for uncorrelated variables, to −1.00 for perfect negative correlation. As an illustration, the heights and weights of adults are positively correlated, tall people tending to be heavier than short people, the actual correlations being .47 for men and .35 for women in the United Kingdom, and similar figures have been reported in the United States and other countries.

A correlation does not necessarily imply causation. If two variables *A* and *B* are shown to be significantly correlated, then it is always possible that *A* causes *B*, that *B* causes *A*, or that *A* and *B* are both caused by some third factor *X*. The only method of establishing causal effects with confidence is by manipulating the conjectured cause (called the independent variable because it is manipulated independently of all other variables) and observing the effects on the variable of interest (the dependent variable) while controlling all other variables that might affect it (the extraneous or nuisance variables). Such a research study is a controlled experiment, and the implication is that causal effects can be established only by controlled experiments, which will be discussed below. This important insight was first made explicit by the English utilitarian philosopher John Stuart Mill (1806–1873) in the middle of the nineteenth century. Mill showed, in particular, that passively observing that *A* is always followed immediately by *B* does not prove that *A* causes *B*, for if it did, then we should have to conclude not only that day causes night but also that night causes day. Both conclusions are based on the logical fallacy of *post hoc ergo propter hoc* (after this, therefore because of this).

The problem of correlation and causality is illustrated by correlational studies that have been carried out to study the relationship between television violence viewing and aggressive behaviour. The data reveal that people who watch a great deal of television violence tend to behave more aggressively than others, but the correlations are very small (in the region of .2), and even if they were larger they could never establish a causal connection. The correlations *may* be due to television violence causing aggressive behaviour, but there are other possibilities. Perhaps people with aggressive personalities are attracted to violent television programmes, which means in effect that aggression causes television violence viewing rather than the other way round, or perhaps some third factor *X* such as a sensation-seeking personality trait causes people both to behave aggressively and to watch television violence, without any direct causal connection between the two.

An important class of correlational studies are those that use multiple regression. This is a form of correlational research originally put forward in a primitive form in 1877 by the English explorer, amateur scientist, and psychologist Sir Francis Galton (1822–1911). It is a technique for analysing the joint and separate influences of two or more predictor variables on a single dependent variable. The general procedure is to work out the correlation between the dependent variable and several predictor variables that might affect it in order to see which have the strongest effects. For example, multiple regression studies of aggressive behaviour in schoolchildren have found numerous predictor variables apart from television violence viewing that are correlated with aggressive behaviour, including sex, age, social class, personality, parental influences, and several others. The results of multiple regression studies are sometimes displayed graphically in path diagrams with points representing variables and lines between them representing correlations, each line being labelled with the size of the correlation between the two variables that it connects. Multiple regression using path diagrams is sometimes called path analysis or structural equation modelling.

Quasi-experiments

There is no precise definition of a quasi-experiment. Roughly speaking, it is any empirical investigation of a cause–effect relationship that is not strictly experimental either because the investigator does not manipulate the independent variable directly and/or because the extraneous variables that might also influence the results are not fully controlled. Because of this imperfect manipulation and/or control, the results of a quasi-experiment cannot be interpreted with as much confidence as those of a controlled experiment, but certain conclusions can sometimes be drawn none the less.

One of the most common quasi-experimental research designs is the non-equivalent groups design in which the investigator does not manipulate the independent variable independently of all other variables but compares existing groups that differ on it. In this research design, the groups may differ in many other ways apart from the independent variable under investigation, and this limits the confidence with which the results can be interpreted. A typical example was discussed in the answer to Question 4 of the quiz in connection with the effects of age on the ability to solve problems involving the conservation of substance. The design problem in that case was that the causal factor of interest was children's level of cognitive development, which cannot be manipulated independently by the investigator. However, level of cognitive development depends largely on age, and the investigator can therefore control it indirectly by comparing the problem-solving abilities of children of different ages. But children of different ages differ in other ways apart from their age-dependent levels of cognitive development – for example, younger children are generally less well educated. It is impossible for the investigator to hold education and all other extraneous variables constant while comparing the thought processes of children of different ages, in other words, the investigator cannot compare children who differ in their levels of cognitive development but are identical in all other respects. It is none the less possible to study the thought processes of children in various carefully specified age ranges, using objective measures of conservation ability.

Studies of this kind are called quasi-experiments because of the incomplete manipulation or control of the relevant variables. The results of quasi-experiments are not as conclusive as those of controlled experiments, and they need to be treated with caution. In many cases, common sense bids us to accept the conclusions as valid. For example, in Piaget's conservation studies, the failure of young children on conservation tasks seems likely to be due to cognitive immaturity. But in other cases serious problems of interpretation arise.

A notorious example of a non-equivalent groups design leading to problems of interpretation is the evidence concerning differences in intelligence between ethnic groups, notably between black and white Americans. Numerous studies have shown that black Americans score, on average, about 15 points below their white compatriots on standardized IQ tests. Some psychologists have argued that the IQ gap is due largely to genetic differences between the two groups, but others believe that it can be explained by environmental factors. It is impossible to perform a controlled experiment to test the genetic hypothesis because it is impossible to separate the genetic factors from the environmental ones. A controlled experiment on this question would involve assigning "black" and "white" genes to a group of new-born infants, exposing them to identical environmental influences for a number of years, and then measuring their IQs. Because such an experiment is manifestly impossible to carry out, ideological considerations tend to influence interpretations of the existing correlational evidence on this question.

In quasi-experimental research it is sometimes possible to control one or more of the extraneous variables indirectly, by statistical techniques, after the data have been collected. An instructive example is an investigation published in 1975 into the personality characteristics of women who develop breast cancer. A group of 160 women with breast tumours were interviewed and given a number of personality tests on the day before they underwent operations to discover whether or not their tumours were malignant (cancerous). At the time of testing, neither the women with the tumours nor the investigators knew which tumours were malignant. After the operation, 69 of the women were found to have breast cancer and 91 were found to have non-malignant tumours. The investigators then compared the personality profiles of the two groups. The most significant difference turned out to be the women's characteristic mode of expressing anger. Among the "extreme suppressors", who virtually never expressed anger openly, and the "extreme expressors", who had a history of frequent outbursts of temper, 67 per cent had malignant tumours, whereas among the women who expressed anger "normally" only 23 per cent had malignant tumours. Statistical analysis (to be discussed later) showed that a difference as large as that is very unlikely to arise by chance, which means that the results are statistically significant. But are the results psychologically significant? Do they suggest a causal link between personality and breast cancer? Because the research used a quasi-experimental non-equivalent groups design, this conclusion is uncertain, and the results could be due to any number of extraneous variables. The investigators anticipated this problem and examined one of the most obvious extraneous variables, namely the ages of the women. The women whose tumours were malignant turned out to be older, on average, than those with non-malignant tumours. This implies that the relationship between personality and breast cancer may be entirely due to age: as women grow older, they may become more extreme in their mode of expressing anger and also more likely to develop breast cancer. The investigators therefore controlled for age indirectly by re-analysing the results separately for women in different age groups. The results remained statistically significant even when the effect of age was partialled out in this way. But even with this refinement the study is by no means conclusive in establishing a causal link between personality and breast cancer, because other unknown and uncontrolled extraneous variables may have played a part, and there is no guarantee that they were ruled out by the research design.

Quasi-experimental studies cannot produce conclusive evidence about causal relationships. In some cases, the results are simply uninterpretable. In others, the weakness of the research design relative to controlled experimentation is less of a problem, and reasonably firm conclusions may be justified on common-sense grounds. In any event, psychologists have to learn to live with these research methods whether they like them or not, because conjectures about causal relationships often need to be tested in circumstances in which independent manipulation of the conjectured cause or complete control over the extraneous variables is simply not feasible.

Controlled experiments

Controlled experimentation is a uniquely important research method. Its importance has nothing to do with its being more objective or more precise than other methods, as some people believe; in fact, survey methods, quasi-experiments, correlational studies, and even case studies can be extremely objective and precise. What makes controlled experiments uniquely important is their ability to establish cause–effect relationships and to allow significance levels to be established with a degree of confidence that is not possible with any other research method. More than half the questions in the quiz were based on the findings of experimental research.

The essential features of the experimental method are manipulation and control. In order to tease out causal effects, the experimenter manipulates the conjectured causal factor (the independent variable) independently, that is, at the same time controlling *all* extraneous variables that might influence the results. For example, suppose an experimenter wants to test the causal hypothesis that deprivation of rapid eye movement (REM) sleep for several nights causes an increase in subsequent REM (a REM rebound effect), which would suggest that REM sleep fulfils some important biological or psychological function. One simple way to manipulate the independent variable would be to assign people at random to an experimental and a control group, to deprive the experimental group of REM sleep for several nights by waking them whenever they showed rapid eye movements and then allowing them to go back to sleep. Then on subsequent nights the experimenter could compare the amount of REM activity that they showed with the amount of REM activity in a control group not deprived of REM sleep but treated identically in all other respects, including how often they were woken up during the night. Any statistically significant difference that was then observed between the two groups on the dependent variable (the measure of REM activity) could be attributed with confidence to the independent variable, because everything else would have been held constant. Numerous experiments have reported that a REM rebound effect does, in fact, occur.

The importance of control in experimental research can be clarified with an example from the gas laws in physics. Boyle's law predicts that if the volume of a gas is decreased by squeezing it into a smaller space, then its pressure increases proportionally. Charles's law predicts that if the temperature of a gas is increased, then its pressure increases proportionally. Now the important point emerges that it is impossible to test either of these predictions empirically without controlling an extraneous variable. To test Boyle's law, an experimenter must manipulate the independent variable (the volume of the gas) and observe the effects of this manipulation on the dependent variable (pressure), but no firm conclusions can be drawn unless an extraneous variable (temperature) is held constant or controlled. Similarly, Charles's law can be tested only by manipulating the independent variable (temperature) and observing the dependent variable (pressure) while controlling an extraneous variable (volume). These are unusually simple and transparent examples because there are only a few variables that influence the results and their effects are well understood. Problems in psychology are seldom so simple.

In a properly controlled experiment, all extraneous variables are controlled while the independent variable is manipulated, and this is the only way of ensuring that any significant effects that are observed can be attributed to the independent variable. In the case of the gas laws, experimental control is relatively straightforward because the pressure of a gas is determined by only two variables – volume and temperature – and therefore only one (extraneous) variable needs to be controlled while the other is being manipulated. In some psychological experiments (see for example Questions 9 and 11 of the quiz), simple and direct methods of control like these are possible. Occasionally, nature provides the necessary control. For example, in studies of the relative effects of nature and nurture on the development of psychological characteristics psychologists sometimes capitalize on "experiments of nature" arising from the phenomenon of identical twins. Identical twins are formed when a single sperm fertilizes a single egg, which then divides in two and grows into two separate individuals. The individuals have identical genes, and consequently they are necessarily of the same sex and similar to each other in all hereditary characteristics. Any difference between them must be due entirely to environmental causes, and studies of identical twins raised in separate environments are therefore useful for estimating the relative importance of environmental factors on intelligence, personality, and individual differences in general. Twin studies involve a high degree of control, because all extraneous genetic factors are held strictly constant, but they are not fully experimental because the independent variable (environment) is not manipulated independently by the experimenter, and this leads to problems in interpreting the results. To be specific, identical twins are very rarely separated at birth, and when they are they tend to be raised in similar home environments, which confuses the issue considerably and means that psychological similarities between them may be due to their similar environments rather than their shared genes.

There are two major classes of controlled experiments in psychology, namely laboratory experiments and field experiments. Laboratory experiments, by far the more common type, are conducted under laboratory conditions, where the manipulation of independent variables and the control of extraneous variables can be carried out conveniently and efficiently, often with the help of on-line computers. Field experiments, on the other hand, are conducted in natural settings, where naturalistic realism is greater but experimental control more difficult. Most of the experiments described in the answers to the quiz were laboratory experiments, but some of those relating to Question 20 (on helping in emergencies) were field experiments. Field experiments are quite often used in certain areas of social psychology.

Controlled experimentation is the most powerful research method available, but it does not automatically eliminate all problems of interpretation. Three forms of validity need to be considered. First, if an experiment is well designed, then the internal validity of its findings will be high. This means simply that the conclusions drawn from its results will be true within the limitations of the methods and subjects used in the experiment. The second form, called external validity, is the extent to which the conclusions stand up when different methods and subjects are used. In order to establish the external validity of the findings, it is generally necessary to replicate the experiment using different methods and subjects. The third form, called ecological validity, is the confidence with which the conclusions can be generalized to naturally occurring (non-experimental) situations. The three forms of validity form a hierarchy: an experiment may produce results that have high internal but low external and ecological validity, or high internal and external but low ecological validity, but the higher forms are not possible without the lower.

The validity of any experiment depends above all on adequate control of extraneous variables. In psychological experiments, extraneous variables can seldom be controlled directly. The reasons are, first, that the experimenter often has no method of suppressing them, second, that there are usually too many of them, and third that many if not most of them may be unknown to the experimenter. One of the main reasons for the plethora of extraneous variables in psychology is the fact that human beings (and other animals) differ from one another. One litre of oxygen is like any other: it will respond exactly like another when it is compressed or heated. But no two people, not even identical twins, are alike in all respects, and they do not respond identically to similar treatments. This is a serious problem that seems, on the face of it, to rule out the possibility of experimental control in most areas of psychological research. Even if all the variables that make one person behave differently from another were known and understood, how could an experimenter hold all but one of them (the independent variable) constant while performing an experiment? The astonishing answer is that there is a simple technique that enables an experimenter to control all extraneous variables simultaneously with complete rigour. It was discovered by the British statistician Ronald Aylmer Fisher in 1926 and is called randomization. Let me explain how it works with a hypothetical example.

Suppose an investigator wishes to discover which of two methods of teaching children a foreign language is more effective, a method based mainly on oral practice, or one based mainly on written exercises. Assuming that some suitable test is available for assessing the children's knowledge of the foreign language, how ought the investigator to proceed? A straightforward approach would be to find a number of children who have been taught by the oral method and a number who have been taught by the written method, to apply the test to both groups, and to compare the average scores. The trouble with that simple and direct but non-experimental approach is that the results would be difficult or impossible to interpret because of the failure to control for extraneous variables. If one group achieved a higher average score than the other, the difference *might* be a consequence of the different teaching methods, but it might equally well be due to one or more of the uncontrolled extraneous variables. For example, there would be no guarantee that the children in the two groups were equally intelligent, and if they were not, then that difference could account for the results.

It is fairly easy to control for intelligence, of course. The investigator could hold intelligence constant by selecting children so that the two groups were matched from the outset on their IQ scores. If one group still scored higher on the foreign language test, then the investigator might argue that this difference is probably due to the teaching methods. But the weakness of that argument emerges as soon as we realize that there are innumerable other extraneous variables to be considered. The problem is much more complicated than investigating the gas laws in physics, where only a single extraneous variable needs to be taken into account at a time. For example, one of the groups may contain a disproportionate number of children whose parents speak the foreign language, or the average age of one of the groups may be higher than the other. The daunting fact has to be faced that there is an *infinite* list of extraneous variables that could potentially influence children's performance on the foreign language test. Some of them could be controlled by matching groups, but others would be difficult or impossible to control or even to measure. More worryingly still, some important extraneous variables may not even occur to the investigator. In other words, if the investigator used the type of quasi-experimental method that I have been discussing, the results would be ambiguous.

The technique of randomization overcomes this difficulty as follows. The experimenter begins by selecting a number of children representative of the population to which the results should apply and assigns them to two treatment conditions strictly at random, by tossing a coin, for example. The two groups are then treated identically except for the single difference arising from the manipulation of the independent variable that one group is taught by the oral method and the other by the written method. The language test is then applied to the children and the average scores of the two groups are compared.

Almost miraculously, randomization controls at a stroke for IQ differences between the children, parents' knowledge of the foreign language, children's age, and all other extraneous variables *including ones that the investigator has not even considered* – for example, each group will contain roughly the same proportions of boys and girls. In fact, randomization ensures that the two groups will tend to be roughly similar in all respects, and the larger the groups, the more similar they will be. If you do not believe this, then try the following demonstration. Choose a page from a telephone directory and assign all the entries on it to two groups by tossing a coin for each entry. Now work out, separately for each group, the proportion of names containing the letter r, or the proportion of telephone numbers ending in 7, the proportion of addresses in a specified sector of the city, or any other objective characteristic of the entries that you can think of. What you will find is that the two groups are roughly similar, and the larger the groups the more similar they will be.

It is important to understand what randomization does and does not achieve. It does not guarantee that the two groups will be identical in all respects, but merely that they will tend to be roughly similar and crucially that any differences will obey the laws of chance. For example, when children are assigned to treatment groups at random it is possible for most of the girls, or most of the children with high IQs, or most of those whose parents speak the foreign language, to end up in one group *by chance*, but it is improbable, especially if the groups are large, because of the way that chance operates, and the probability can be calculated precisely. Assuming that the experiment is properly controlled, if a difference is found between the groups on the language test, then there are only two possibilities: the difference must be due either to the independent variable (the different teaching methods) or to chance.

That is precisely how statistics comes into psychology. Statistical tests have been devised for the express purpose of enabling researchers to calculate the probability or odds of a particular difference arising by chance. If the probability is small, then the researcher is entitled to feel confident that the difference is due to the independent variable, because that is the only other explanation if the experiment was properly controlled.

Statistics: The basic ideas

People are often surprised or even dismayed to learn that statistics has a part to play in psychology, and some give up the idea of studying psychology for that reason alone. In fact, the level of mathematical ability that is required in psychology is very modest, and there are few who cannot easily master the necessary skills. Academic and professional psychologists, for their part, vary widely in their understanding of statistics. Most get by with only a rudimentary grasp of the fundamental ideas that enables them to apply a handful of simple statistical tests more or less mechanically. They accept on trust that the tests do what they are supposed to do, and when they are faced with statistical problems that cannot be solved by routine or off-the-shelf methods, they simply seek advice from their more mathematically minded colleagues.

An elementary knowledge of statistics is indispensable for making sense of the technical literature of psychology, because research findings are nearly always reported in numerical form and analysed by statistical methods. There are two main branches of statistics, called descriptive statistics and inferential statistics. Descriptive statistics is used to summarize numerical data in ways that make them more easily interpretable, and it involves presenting data in tables and graphs and calculating averages, variabilities, correlations, and so forth. Unemployment statistics, trade statistics, and accident statistics are well-known examples of descriptive statistics, which have been used in psychology ever since Francis Galton applied them in the 1860s to the results of his investigations of intelligence (see chapter 5). Techniques of inferential statistics, on the other hand, are devoted to interpreting data by drawing inferences from samples via statistical tests. These tests are designed to enable researchers to decide whether the results of their experiments are statistically significant or whether similar results could have arisen merely by chance.

The fundamental logic of inferential statistics is devious and slippery, but I think I can explain it. An elementary example should make everything clear. I am going to develop a statistical test from first principles, so that the fundamental ideas are exposed. In the previous section I outlined an experiment to discover which of two teaching methods, oral or written, is more effective in teaching children a foreign language. Let us assume that theory or past research suggests that the oral method will work better, and that an experimenter sets out to test this hypothesis. To keep things simple, imagine that the experimenter uses only six children as research participants or subjects and that three are randomly assigned to each group (oral or written). After assigning subjects to the two groups at random, the experimenter is careful to treat them identically in all respects apart from the manipulation of the independent variable (teaching method). The whole procedure could be automated with the help of a computer and a properly equipped language laboratory. Then each child is given a suitable test to measure the dependent variable (knowledge of the foreign language). Again for simplicity's sake, suppose that the test merely places the six children in rank order, from worst to best, according to their knowledge of the language. Using the letter O to stand for a child taught by the oral method and *W* for one taught by the written method, and arranging the six subjects from worst on the left to best on the right, suppose the results came out like this:

WWOWOO

It seems on the face of it that the oral method worked better, as hypothesized, because most of the children taught by that method are ranked higher than most of those taught by the written method. The three who were taught by the oral method came first, second, and fourth, whereas the three who were taught by the written method came third, fifth and sixth. Of course, differences in age, intelligence, motivation, and so forth are bound to have influenced the results. But we know that these extraneous variables are distributed randomly between the two groups because the subjects were randomly assigned to the groups.

Let us write 1 for the lowest rank (the child who came bottom), 2 for the next rank, and so on up to 6 for the highest rank. What we want to know is whether the ranks achieved under the oral method are significantly higher than those achieved under the written method. The children taught by the oral method get a rank sum of 3 + 5 + 6 = 14, and those taught by the written method get a rank sum of 1 + 2 + 4 = 7. The *O* subjects outranked the *W* subjects by 14 − 7 = 7 ranks, therefore we say that the rank difference is 7. This is a clear difference in favour of the oral method. Could it be due merely to chance? Well, yes, we can never conclusively disprove the possibility that any difference is due to chance. But here, because we used randomization, we can calculate the exact probability of such a large difference occurring by chance.

We need to know the probability of obtaining, by chance alone, a rank difference at least as extreme, in the hypothesized direction (in favour of the oral method), as the one that was actually obtained. There are twenty different ways in which three *O*s and three *W*s can be ranked. To see this clearly, think of arranging three red and three white balls in order, and you will find that there are exactly twenty different arrange-

ments possible. Each of these arrangements is equally likely if the elements are shuffled randomly. Here is a complete list, together with the rank differences (the sum of the O ranks minus the sum of the W ranks):

WWWOOO	WWOWOO	WWOOWO	WOWWOO	WOWOWO
(9)	(7)	(5)	(5)	(3)
OWWWOO	WWOOOW	OWWOWO	WOOWWO	WOWOOW
(3)	(3)	(1)	(1)	(1)
OWOWWO	WOOWOW	OWWOOW	OOWWWO	OWOWOW
(−1)	(−1)	(−1)	(−3)	(−3)
WOOOWW	OOWWOW	OWOOWW	OOWOWW	OOOWWW
(−3)	(−5)	(−5)	(−7)	(−9)

It is obvious from this table that among the twenty equally likely arrangements only two (the first two in the top row) are at least as extreme in the hypothesized direction as the results actually obtained; all the rest have lower rank differences. The probability of obtaining, by chance alone, results as extreme as those obtained in the experiment is therefore exactly 2/20, or 10 per cent. This means that if the independent variable (the difference in teaching methods) had no effect at all on the dependent variable, and if the experiment were to be repeated many times, results as extreme in favour of the oral method as those actually obtained would occur by chance in approximately 10 per cent of the experiments. In other words, the results do not allow us to conclude with great confidence that the teaching methods that were used in the experiment made any difference. By convention, psychologists usually call an experimental outcome statistically significant if the chance probability is less than 5 per cent. According to that convention, the results of the experiment are not statistically significant. In fact, with so few subjects, the only pattern that is on the margin of the 5 per cent significance level is *WWWOOO*, which represents exactly 5 per cent (1 out of 20) of the equally probable outcomes in the table.

What I have just described is the Mann–Whitney U test. When the samples are larger, researchers do not laboriously list all the equally likely outcomes and then count them as I did, because the number of outcomes becomes very large as the sample size increases. Instead, they simply apply a stock formula which does the counting for them, and then they look up the probability level in a table. The results of most psychological investigations are analysed with a small number of simple statistical tests that are versatile and powerful though easy to use. The logic of all these tests is essentially the same. Every statistical significance test starts by assuming that the independent variable had no effect and that any difference found on the dependent variable is therefore due to chance. This is called the null hypothesis. The alternative hypothesis or experimental hypothesis is the experimenter's hypothesis that the independent variable caused some specified difference. The test calculates the probability of obtaining, by chance alone, a difference at least as extreme as the one actually obtained, and this probability is called the significance level. If the significance level is sufficiently small – usually less than 5 per cent – then the experimenter rejects the null hypothesis and attributes the results to the alternative hypothesis. If the experiment is properly controlled, then aside from chance the alternative hypothesis is the only other possible explanation for the difference. On the other hand, if the significance level is not low enough, then no firm conclusions can be drawn and the results are said to be non-significant.

That is the logic of null hypothesis testing. Its importance arises from the need for objective criteria of the significance of research data. It adds considerable weight to the conclusions that can be inferred from numerical results, as the following example will show.

A crime in Jung's asylum   On 6 February 1908 a theft was reported at an asylum for the insane in Zürich, Switzerland. A nurse had left a leather purse in a wardrobe in her room. It contained some money, a silver watch-chain, a stencil for marking the asylum's kitchen utensils, and a receipt from Dosenbach's Shoe Shop, and the purse had mysteriously disappeared during the afternoon. The incident came to the attention of a staff member of the asylum, the famous Swiss psychoanalyst Carl Gustav Jung (1875–1961), who immediately took up the challenge of trying to solve the crime using his new word-association test as a lie detector. He prepared a list of thirty-seven critical words such as *watch, chain, leather, stencil,* and *Dosenbach* that were intimately associated with the crime, although only a person with guilty knowledge could recognize their significance. He mixed these critical words up with sixty-three innocent words, and then he read the words out to each of the suspect nurses in turn. Each suspect had to respond to each word with the first thought that came into her mind, and Jung took note of "complex indicators" such as abnormally long reaction times, multiple responses, repetitions of the stimulus word, and meaningless associations. He then read out the list a second time, and the suspect tried to remember her original responses.

Jung considered imperfect reproductions to be complex indicators of special importance, and he pronounced one of the suspects guilty mainly on the basis of her imperfect reproductions. To the 63 innocent words she gave 15 imperfect and 48 perfect reproductions, but to the 37 critical words associated with the crime, she gave 19 imperfect and 18 perfect reproductions. Inferential statistics was in its infancy in 1908, and Jung did not calculate the significance level of his results, but he thought that the imperfect reproductions to the critical words "surpass by far the expected.... One may venture to designate such a subject as probably guilty." The suspect soon broke down and confessed, and Jung commented: "Thus the success of the experiment was confirmed.... There is much in experimental psychology which is less useful." A simple statistical test called Fisher's exact probability test confirms Jung's guess. It turns out that the null hypothesis, that the suspect's imperfect reproductions were distributed randomly between the critical and innocent words, can be rejected at the 1 per cent significance level. This means that a distribution as incriminating as the one in question would happen by chance less than once in a hundred repetitions. It is reasonable to reject the null hypothesis in favour of the alternative hypothesis that she was guilty, and we have more justification for this conclusion than Jung had. The next two examples will show how fallible intuitive judgements of probability can be.

Deaths from horse kicks
Over a 19-year period from 1875 to 1894, 122 men in 200 Prussian army corps died as a result of horse kicks. Assuming that such accidents strike at random, how would you expect the 122 deaths to be distributed among the 200 corps? The actual distribution seemed

unmistakably non-random to many people: 109 corps experienced no deaths from horse kicks, 26 experienced more than one such accident, and one corps experienced no fewer than four. These findings played a large part in the development of a spurious theory of accident-proneness. A technique called the binomial test allows us to work out the distribution of deaths that is most likely on the basis of chance alone. The observed and expected distributions are as follows:

Number of deaths	0	1	2	3	4
Observed number of corps	109	65	22	3	1
Expected numbers of corps	109	66	20	4	1

Many people feel intuitively that the most likely distribution is for each of the 122 deaths to occur in a different corps. In fact, the probability of this even distribution is roughly one in 10,000,000,000,000,000,000,000, in other words it would be a miracle.

Jury verdicts In the case *Johnson* v. *Louisiana* in 1972, the United States Supreme Court ruled that a twelve-member jury, required to reach a verdict by a majority of at least nine votes to three, is no more likely to convict than a five-member jury that has to be unanimous. Johnson was convicted of robbery by a nine-to-three majority of a twelve-member jury. He argued that, other things being equal, a five-member unanimous jury (used in Louisiana for less serious crimes) was less likely to have convicted him. The court rejected the appeal:

> If the appellant's position is that it is easier to convince nine of 12 jurors than to convince all of five, he is simply challenging the judgment of the Louisiana Legislature. That body obviously intended to vary the difficulty of proving guilt with the gravity of the offense and the severity of the punishment. We remain unconvinced by anything the appellant has presented that this legislative judgment was defective in any constitutional sense.
>
> (*Johnson* v. *Louisiana*, 406 U.S. 356, 1972, pp. 364–365)

The simplest way to challenge the judgement of the Louisiana Legislature, and that of the United States Supreme Court as well, is by calculating the probability that a five-member jury, drawn at random from a twelve-member jury with a nine-to-three majority,

would contain five members in favour of conviction. This test can be done from first principles, starting with rules about ordering (how many different ways can x things be arranged in order, or how many different queues can two, three, four, or x people form?). It turns out that, of all the five-member juries that can be selected from among the twelve jurors, more than 84 per cent have at least one member who votes against conviction. In other words, if one such jury were to be chosen at random from among the original twelve jurors who convicted Johnson, and assuming that the jurors all stuck to their original votes, the probability is less than .16 that it would have convicted him.

The examples I have discussed show that intuitive judgements of probability can be unreliable. The safest way of determining the significance of an experimental outcome is by applying an appropriate statistical test. The need for statistics arises whenever, as is usually the case, the results are not quite clear-cut or, to put it another way, when they do not speak for themselves. Similar problems of interpretation arise in agricultural and medical research, nuclear physics, and many other branches of science. Ever since the 1930s it has been customary to analyse such results with the techniques of inferential statistics. The calculations are usually done on computers, for which packages of standard statistical tests are available as software. A little knowledge of statistics goes a long way in psychology. But the mechanical and unquestioning approach to statistics adopted by many people can lead to serious errors, and it fails completely when the data do not fit any of the standard tests. An understanding of the ideas behind the tests is therefore highly desirable, and it enables new problems to be tackled from first principles. If you have read this chapter carefully, you should understand the logic of null hypothesis statistical testing and its inextricable relation to experimental design.

Further reading

Four good books on qualitative research methods are Uwe Flick's *An introduction to qualitative research* (London: Sage, 1998); Nicky Hayes's *Doing qualitative analysis in psychology* (Hove: Psychology Press, 1997); Mary Kopala and Lisa A. Suzuki's *Using qualitative methods in psychology* (Thousand Oaks, CA: Sage, 1998); and Steven J. Taylor and Robert Brogdan's *Introduction to qualitative research methods: A guidebook and resource* (New York: Wiley, 1998).

The case study in which Freud first presented his theory of paranoia can be found in his *Collected papers*, authorized and translated by A. and J. Strachey, Volume III (London: Hogarth, 1948, pp. 387–470). The experiment designed to test Freud's theory of paranoia was reported by P.G. Datson in an article entitled "Perception of homosexual words in paranoid schizophrenia" (*Perceptual and Motor Skills, 6*, 45–55, 1956).

The randomized response technique of survey research was introduced by Stanley L. Warner in an article entitled "Randomized response: A survey technique for eliminating evasive answer bias" (*Journal of the American Statistical Association 60*, 63–69, 1965).

The correlation between people's heights and weights comes from a fully representative survey of 10,000 men and women in Great Britain reported by I. Knight (*The heights and weights of adults in Great Britain*, London: Her Majesty's Stationery Office, 1984). The investigation of the personality characteristics of women with breast cancer was reported by S. Greer and T. Morris in a paper entitled "Psychological attributes of women who develop breast cancer: A controlled study" (*Journal of Psychosomatic Research, 19*, 147–153, 1975). The REM rebound effect was first reported by William Dement in an article entitled "The effect of dream deprivation" (*Science, 131*, 1705–1707, 1960). The logic of randomized experimentation was originally worked out by Ronald A. Fisher, whose *The design of experiments* (8th ed.) (London: Oliver & Boyd, 1966) is a classic. A detailed discussion of widely used research methods can be found in Donald T. Campbell and Julian C. Stanley's *Experimental and quasi-experimental designs for research* (Chicago: Rand McNally, 1966) and in Thomas D. Cook and Donald T. Campbell's *Quasi-experimentation: Design and analysis issues for field settings* (Chicago: Rand McNally, 1979). There are many good textbooks of statistics, including Robert R. Pagano's *Understanding statistics in the behavioral sciences* (5th ed., Pacific Grove, CA: Brooks/Cole, 1998) and David C. Howell's *Fundamental statistics for the behavioral sciences* (4th ed., Pacific Grove, CA: Duxbury, 1998). Finally, a collection of introductory expositions of research methods and statistics can be found in the following book edited by me: Andrew M. Colman (Ed.), *Psychological research methods and statistics* (London and New York: Longman, 1995).

Chapter 5

The origins and development of psychology

History helps us to understand the present. We cannot comprehend any subject deeply without knowing something about its historical background. This book would therefore be incomplete without a brief account of the origins and development of psychology, and it is a fascinating story in itself. Instead of reciting the usual catalogue of Great Men that so often passes for historiography, I shall try to trace the evolution of a few key ideas.

Psychology has been recognized as an independent discipline for a little over a hundred years, but speculations about psychological matters can be found in the records of most ancient civilizations. Even experimental methods were occasionally used in ancient times to answer psychological questions. The earliest account of a psychological experiment is contained in *The Histories* of Herodotus (?485–?425 BC), the world's first history book, completed in about 429 BC. The experiment was performed by the ancient Egyptian Pharaoh Psammetichus I (664–610 BC) in the seventh century BC to determine whether human beings have an inborn capacity for speech, and if so, which particular language is innate. He ordered two infants to be brought up in a remote place by a shepherd who was forbidden to speak in their presence. After two years the children began to speak, and the word that they repeated most often was *becos*, which turned out to be the Phrygian word for bread. Psammetichus concluded that the capacity for speech is inborn and that the innate, natural language of human beings is Phrygian. The questions to which the experiment was addressed seem naïve and risible today, and the experiment was poorly designed – even some of Psammetichus's contemporaries pointed out that the children may merely have been imitating the bleating of goats. But it was a psychological experiment none the less, and in its conceptual structure and methodology it is remarkably similar to modern experiments in which birds have been reared in isolation from members of their own species in order to discover which features of their songs are innate.

If the story is true, and it should be mentioned that Herodotus was not the most reliable of historians, the Egyptian experiment was certainly a rare exception. Empirical methods based on observation and experiment were seldom used to answer psychological problems until comparatively recently. Before psychology emerged as an independent discipline in Germany in the late nineteenth century, it existed for a long time as a branch of philosophy called mental philosophy to distinguish it from natural philosophy, now called physics. During the eighteenth and nineteenth centuries, developments in the biological sciences began to suggest empirical approaches to some of the problems of mental philosophy, and towards the end of the nineteenth century psychology finally reached maturity and gained its independence as a separate discipline in its own right. Thus although psychology is barely a century old as an independent discipline, psychological speculation, practice, and even empirical research clearly have much older pedigrees. That is what the German psychologist Hermann von Ebbinghaus (1850–1909) meant when he wrote in 1908 that "psychology has a long past but a short history", although the remark is more often quoted than understood. Before discussing its short history, I shall outline its long philosophical and biological past.

Philosophical roots

Systematic advances in psychological knowledge began in ancient Greece with the pre-Socratic philosophers of the sixth and fifth centuries BC. In about 585 BC, Thales of Miletus (?624–?564 BC) and his followers were the first to realize that the brain plays a crucial role in mental experience, in spite of the fact that emotions give rise to physical sensations in the chest and stomach rather than the head. In particular, they understood that the eyes and ears cannot see and hear on their own without some form of internal representation, which they correctly located in the brain. In addition to this, they were the first to develop theories to explain the fact that people differ not only in appearance but also in temperament, or what psychologists later called personality. The doctrine of the four temperaments, uncertainly attributed to the Greek physician and father of medicine Hippocrates (?460–?377 BC) and widely accepted throughout the Middle Ages, classified people as sanguine (optimistic), melancholic (depressive), choleric (short-tempered), or phlegmatic (apathetic) according to the supposed balance in their bodies of four humours or fluids called blood (*sanguis*), black bile (*melaina chole*), yellow bile (*chole*), and phlegm (*phlegma*). The physiological basis of the theory was undermined during the Renaissance by advances in biological knowledge, but the underlying typology survived in some modern personality theories. The importance of the pre-Socratics in the history of psychology lies not so much in the answers that they gave, but in the fact that they thought to ask the questions in the first place.

From a modern vantage point, what is most striking about the psychology of the pre-Socratics is not what they included but what they excluded, in particular the absence of any concept of an individual soul or mind. The pre-Socratics understood the difference between inanimate objects and living things, and they had a concept of soul to explain the difference, but they believed that this soul was diffused through all living things. It was Aristotle (384–322 BC) who first popularized the idea of individual souls in his treatise *De Anima* (Concerning the Soul), the world's first and most influential textbook of psychology, in about 350 BC. Aristotle believed that every living body possesses a soul that gives it life, and that a living body and its soul cannot exist without each other. He classified individual souls in order of merit, from the merely nutritive and reproductive souls of plants, through the sensitive souls of animals – sensitive inasmuch as they possessed the five classical senses of vision, hearing, smell, taste, and touch that Aristotle enumerated in this book – to the rational souls of human beings.

For over a thousand years, from about AD 400 until 1450, the intellectual life of Europe was dominated by Christian theology. The doctrine of the individual soul was of central importance in medieval thinking, but the overriding religious dogma was that people are subject to the inexorable will of God, and the Church discouraged objective investigations of behaviour and mental experience. Near the beginning of the medieval period a few independently minded thinkers continued to speculate about psychological matters. For example, Saint Augustine (AD 354–430), the bishop of Hippo in North Africa, gave interesting analyses of his own stream of consciousness and of the psychological development of children, and he also anticipated Sigmund Freud

(1856–1939) by suggesting that slips of the tongue may reveal inner conflicts and by putting forward the remarkable theory that avarice is caused by sexual repression. But throughout the Dark Ages following the fall of Rome in AD 476 the development of psychological thought was at a virtual standstill as all prudent people concentrated on saving their souls rather than studying them.

The first important thinker of the post-medieval period was the French philosopher René Descartes (1596–1650). His importance in the history of psychology derived chiefly from his theory about the relationship between mind and body. He was the first major philosopher to distinguish clearly between mental experiences such as thoughts, feelings, sensations, and emotions on the one hand, and physical processes such as the internal workings of the body and outward behaviour on the other. He considered the human body to be a machine that operates according to ordinary physical laws. He placed mental experiences in a separate category and interpreted them as the work of the soul. According to Descartes the soul is immaterial because it does not occupy space like a physical object and is not subject to the restrictions of physical laws. In other words, Descartes pioneered the notion of "the ghost in the machine".

Philosophers had been speculating since classical times about the location of mental experiences. Where do thoughts, feelings, sensations, emotions, dreams, and so forth take place? The pre-Socratics plumped for the brain. The later and more influential Greek philosopher Plato (?427–?347 BC) located desire in the liver, courage in the heart, and only reason in the brain. Plato's pupil Aristotle strayed even further from the target by declaring the heart to be the seat of all mental experiences. For Descartes, mental experiences are functions of the soul and, because the soul is immaterial, they cannot be located in any particular organ of the body. But this created a puzzle. It seemed obvious to Descartes that the soul and the body somehow manage to influence each other, and this suggests that they must interact somewhere. A mental experience such as a desire to eat can have physical effects such as a flow of saliva and a movement of one's hand towards a bowl of fruit, and conversely a physical event such as an object falling on one's foot can cause a mental experience such as a sensation of pain. Mental and physical events clearly influence each other, and this seems to imply that they must interact somewhere in the body.

Descartes knew that all information gathered by the sense organs is transmitted to the brain. He therefore narrowed his search for the seat of soul–body interaction to the brain, and he eventually identified a part of the brain called the pineal gland as the organ of interaction. The pineal gland, a pea-sized structure shaped like a miniature pine cone, seemed an obvious choice for three reasons. First, it is attached to the base of the brain in the very centre of the head. Second, Descartes believed that only human beings possess rational souls, and the evidence at his disposal suggested that they are also the only creatures blessed with pineal glands, although we now know this to be untrue. Third and most important, the pineal gland is the only part of the main structure of the brain that is not divided into two halves. When images from the two eyes are perceived by the soul, they are fused together into a single picture, and the pineal gland seemed to Descartes to be the only part of the brain capable of performing this feat of integration. If the seat of soul–body interaction were anywhere else in the brain, we should all suffer from permanent double vision. For all these reasons the pineal gland was the natural choice. The precise manner of its operation was another question, to which Descartes' answer was rather vague. He suggested that the pineal gland operates like a valve, controlling the flow of "vital spirits" through the body, and that these vital spirits somehow enable the soul and body to influence each other.

Descartes' theory did not seem to later generations of philosophers, or even to some of his own contemporaries, to be a convincing solution to the problem. Mental experiences and physical processes seem to belong to quite separate realms. A mental experience like grief can be accompanied by a physical process like weeping, but grief seems to belong to an altogether different category from anything physical. How can a mental experience that exists outside the physical world have an effect on the purely physical body, and vice versa? To put it plainly, how can a thought move a muscle, and how can sticks and stones bruise a soul? This is the nub of the mind–body problem that has tormented philosophers ever since the seventeenth century. The various attempts to solve it profoundly influenced the early development of psychology.

Descartes accepted the common-sense view that mind and body do indeed influence each other. This view is nowadays called interactionism. His English contemporary Thomas Hobbes (1588–1679) tried to slither out of the problem by claiming that only physical matter exists, and that mental experiences are merely a form of "matter in motion" in the nerves and the brain. Descartes' common-sense interactionism does not really solve the problem either. In fact, it could be argued that Descartes did not show any evidence of even having understood the problem until it was explained to him by Princess Elizabeth of Bohemia (1596–1662), the daughter of King James I of England and VI of Scotland. The story is worth telling to put Descartes' contribution in perspective. In 1643, Princess Elizabeth wrote a letter to Descartes. She had read his *Meditations on First Philosophy* and had grasped the full significance of the mind–body problem immediately. In her letter, she summarized the problem simply and clearly and requested an answer from Descartes. Descartes began his reply by admitting that he had not dealt with the problem in his book, and he offered a waffly and incomprehensible explanation in terms of gravity, a very fashionable and difficult scientific concept at that time, before Newton clarified it. Princess Elizabeth refused to be fobbed off so easily. "I cannot understand", she wrote in a second letter, "the way that the soul, unextended and immaterial, moves the body, in terms of the idea you used to have about gravity ... or why the soul is so much governed by the body, when it ... has nothing in common with it." Descartes conceded in reply that he understood soul–body interaction "only in an obscure way" and commented that "those who never do philosophize and make use only of their senses have no doubt that the soul moves the body and the body acts on the soul". He expressed his "sincere admiration" for her Highness's intelligence, admitting that his explanation in terms of gravity had been "lame", and concluded patronizingly by warning her that, although it was fine to think about philosophical problems occasionally, "it would be very harmful to occupy one's intellect often by meditating on them". On the basis of this exchange of letters, I believe that historians should consider giving Princess Elizabeth credit for discovering the mind–body problem, traditionally attributed to Descartes, the "father of modern philosophy".

Following Descartes, the eighteenth century, often called the Age of Reason, was an era during which a critical and rational approach to the world of ideas flourished. The intellectual optimism of the eighteenth century was largely a consequence of the dazzling successes recently achieved in the physical sciences by Galileo (1564–1642), Kepler (1571–1630), and eventually Newton (1642–1727). But, curiously enough, these were lean times in the history of psychology. To understand why mental philosophy was neglected while natural philosophy thrived as never before, we must try to imagine the extraordinary impact of Newton's theory of mechanics. Newton put forward his theory towards the end of the seventeenth century. It was, and still is, the boldest and most successful theory in the entire history of science. It consists of just four postulates, simple enough to be understood by a child, that explain not only the apples falling on people's heads, but also the ebb and flow of tides and the peculiar motions of the planets, moons, and comets in the solar system. The motions of these objects can be predicted from Newton's theory with a degree of accuracy that is almost beyond belief. In 1859 astronomers discovered that the planet Mercury drifts from the predicted orbit by 43 seconds of arc, or roughly one hundredth of a degree, *per century*, which shows that Newton's theory is indeed an oversimplification. In 1916 Einstein (1879–1955) developed a general theory of relativity that removed this imperfection.

The impression created by the almost miraculous success of Newtonian mechanics was that before long natural science would be able to explain everything. During the eighteenth century, most educated people felt that a complete understanding of the universe in terms of matter in motion was just around the corner. The existing body of scientific knowledge was so powerful that the only tasks left for science seemed relatively straightforward matters of filling in missing details here and there. The laws of mechanics were assumed to be capable of solving all remaining scientific problems.

In France, where Descartes' influence had been strongest, the search began for a solution to the mind–body problem more in keeping with the spirit of the times. The *philosophes* of the Enlightenment – the period leading up to the French Revolution of 1789 – began to lean towards materialism. French intellectuals were fully aware of Newton's achievements across the English Channel, especially after Voltaire (1694–1778) returned from a period of exile in England and wrote rave reviews of Newton's work in the French press. A new solution to the mind–body problem with a strongly physical bias became fashionable in France. The new idea was summed up by the phrase *L'Homme machine* (The Human Machine), the title of a book by La Mettrie (1709–1751) that was published in 1748.

The French materialists were not thoroughgoing in their materialism. Even La Mettrie, whose views were considered radical, stopped short of suggesting that reality consists only of physical objects and processes, or that mental experiences are not real. The *philosophes* proposed instead a diluted version of materialism that came to be called epiphenomenalism. According to this doctrine, mental experiences are real, but they are merely trivial by-products or epiphenomena of one particular class of physical processes, namely brain processes. In other words, they are real but unimportant, like the smoke rising above a factory. The implication of this theory is that physical processes can cause mental experiences, but mental experiences, because they are mere epiphenomena, cannot have physical effects. In place of the two-way interactionism of Descartes, the French materialists substituted a one-way body–mind interactionism: a heavy object falling on one's foot can cause a mental experience of pain, but a thought cannot move a muscle.

The doctrine of epiphenomenalism had a damaging effect on the development of mental philosophy during the Enlightenment. Serious thinkers began to consider mental experiences to be unimportant and uninteresting. If thoughts and feelings are mere epiphenomena, and if they cannot have any effects of their own, then they seem hardly worth investigating. And if they must be investigated, then the only valid approach is to study the machinery of the nervous system, and especially the brain, from which they arise. These prejudices gained a firm foothold during the eighteenth-century Enlightenment, first in France and later throughout Europe, and it is partly because of their effects that psychology is such a young science. It was only after the epiphenomenalist solution to the mind–body problem went into decline that psychology was able to come out of hibernation and grow into an independent discipline.

Although French materialism was largely to blame for the popularity of epiphenomenalism and the resulting neglect of psychological problems, it had an invigorating effect on other fields of research that later contributed to the development of psychology. Biological research, especially the branch of biology devoted to human physiology, thrived in the climate of French materialism. Many important discoveries about the sense organs, the nervous system, and the brain emerged from laboratories in France and Britain. There were also important developments in the field of medicine that were later to have repercussions in psychology. During the 1770s the Viennese physician Franz Anton Mesmer (1734–1815) introduced the scientific community in Paris to his work on "animal magnetism". This was a substance resembling ordinary magnetism that he claimed to have discovered in human bodies and that could be channelled, stored, and transmitted between people. Patients suffering from a variety of symptoms sat around a wooden tub filled with water, iron filings, and glass. Metal rods protruding from the lid of the tub were applied to their afflicted parts while Mesmer moved among them, making passes over their bodies and occasionally touching them with a long iron wand. Patients often fell into convulsions as a result of animal magnetism, and many declared themselves cured after a few sessions. Although Mesmer never actually hypnotized anyone, the practice of mesmerism formed the basis of later research into hypnosis.

Another consequence of materialist thinking was an entirely new way of looking at insanity. Since medieval times, insanity had been interpreted as a manifestation of spirit possession, and its unfortunate victims were executed, chained up in prisons, or tortured to exorcize evil spirits from their bodies and save their souls. Materialist thinkers reinterpreted insanity as a kind of illness, caused by presumed physical disorders of the brain and nervous system, that called for medical rather than spiritual treatment. This approach to insanity, which was entirely novel, led the French psychiatrist Philippe Pinel (1745–1826) to unchain the insane in the dungeons of the Parisian madhouses in 1793, and executions for witchcraft virtually came to an end throughout Europe.

During the early nineteenth century, the doctrine of epiphenomenalism gradually lost its appeal. The main reason for its decline was its inability to assimilate certain facts that came to light during that period. In particular, brain research seemed unable to explain mental experiences, even as epiphenomena, mesmerism turned out to have no physical basis, and mental disorders were discovered that were not caused by physical disorders of the brain or nervous system.

The most active field of brain research in the early decades of the nineteenth century was a strange mixture of science and pseudoscience called phrenology. Its founder, the German physiologist Franz Joseph Gall (1758–1828), believed that every mental faculty is located in a specific region of the brain. The most highly developed mental faculties were supposed to be associated with enlargements of the brain, visible as bumps on the skull, in thirty-seven key brain regions. Gall and his disciple Johann Kaspar Spurzheim

(1809–1872) tried to prove this theory by examining the skulls of inmates of prisons and insane asylums. For example, they reported that pickpockets had prominent bumps on the skull in the region associated with the faculty of acquisitiveness. When Gall died, his skull was examined by one of his followers, who reported that "the organs of ... Adhesiveness, Combativeness, and Destructiveness were all very well developed in Gall. His Secretiveness was also rather large, but he never made use of it." Gall was thus hoist with his own phrenological petard, but his theory continued to enjoy enormous popularity, especially in Britain, where at one time no fewer than twenty-nine phrenological societies flourished, and in the United States. French biologists and medical experts were sceptical about phrenology from the start, and accumulating scientific evidence gradually proved them right. Phrenology collapsed, and to the embarrassment of epiphenomenalism, no simple relationship between brain anatomy and mental faculties was found.

The second blow to epiphenomenalism was the decline of animal magnetism. In 1784 the King of France appointed two commissions to investigate the work of Mesmer and his followers. The members included the astronomer Bailly, the chemist Lavoisier, the physician Guillotin (after whom a notorious method of execution was named), and the inventor Benjamin Franklin, who was then United States Ambassador to France. The commissioners performed several experiments, and these experiments led them to the conclusion that animal magnetism did not exist and that the effects of mesmerism were due to touch, imagination, and imitation. Thoroughly discredited, Mesmer left Paris the following year and disappeared into obscurity. Research into hypnosis continued, but the physical theory of animal magnetism on which it was based was gradually abandoned. By the beginning of the nineteenth century it had become apparent that hypnosis was a purely psychological process rather than an epiphenomenon of some mysterious physical substance. It was a dramatic example of a psychological process that could have important bodily effects, something that was impossible according to the doctrine of epiphenomenalism. But the evidence was clear: for example, in the early part of the nineteenth century the English surgeon James Esdaile (1808–1859) performed literally hundreds of major operations in India using hypnotic anaesthesia.

The third serious problem for epiphenomenalism was the discovery of mental disorders that could not be traced to physical causes. The most striking examples were cases of hysteria in which patients suffered blindness, deafness, paralysis, or loss of sensation without any apparent organic disorder. As knowledge about the nervous system accumulated, it became clear that physical causes could be ruled out in at least some cases. A typical example was glove anaesthesia, a condition characterized by absence of sensation or feeling in the hand, the anaesthetic area ending abruptly at the wrist. The distribution of sensory nerves allows no possible neurological cause of the symptom, because the sensory nerve that supplies the hand also supplies the lower arm, yet cases of hysterical glove anaesthesia were often reported. Hysteria and other mental disorders gradually came to be viewed in a similar way to hypnosis, as essentially psychological in origin and nature, but having bodily effects. This interpretation was difficult to reconcile with epiphenomenalism. The mind–body problem was back with a vengeance.

At about the same time, the common-sense idea that mind can influence matter came up against a new difficulty. The problem arose from the discovery of the first law of thermodynamics, which used to be called the law of conservation of energy. It was discovered by a German physician, Julius Mayer (1814–1878), who tried to publish it in the leading physics journal *Annalen der Physik* but was forced to publish it in an obscure chemistry journal after it was rejected by the editors of the physics journal. As a result, it was ignored by physicists when it eventually appeared. Deeply distressed, Mayer suffered a mental breakdown from which he never recovered. Meanwhile, the law was independently rediscovered in England by William Thomson (1824–1907), later to become Lord Kelvin, who presented it to the Royal Society in 1851 and was credited with its discovery.

The essence of the first law of thermodynamics asserts that when a system changes from one state to another, energy is converted to a different form but the total amount of energy remains unchanged or is conserved. Heat, chemical reactions, electricity, and magnetism can all be converted into mechanical energy, but energy cannot be created out of nothing. Every physical movement or change in the world involves a transfer of energy. All physical work consumes one form of energy and generates an equal amount of energy of another form. For example, rubbing one's hands together consumes food energy and generates mechanical energy and heat. The crucial point is that the total amount of energy in the universe remains constant through all these changes. The discovery of this law led to the conclusion that a physical movement of the body, such as walking, writing, or rubbing one's hands together, cannot be caused by a mental processes such as a thought or a desire, because mental processes do not belong to the physical realm of heat, chemical reactions, electricity, and magnetism. Bodily movements involve mechanical work, a form of energy that cannot come from a non-physical source without violating the first law.

The decline of epiphenomenalism and the discovery of the first law of thermodynamics forced nineteenth-century philosophers to find a new solution to the mind–body problem. The solution that became fashionable was called psycho-physical parallelism. The idea had been mooted by the German philosopher and mathematician Gottfried Wilhelm von Leibniz (1646–1716) in the early eighteenth century, but Leibniz was a century ahead of his time, and his idea caught on only in the mid nineteenth century when the intellectual climate was more receptive to it for the reasons outlined above.

The fundamental idea behind psycho-physical parallelism can be explained quite simply. Mental experiences are accompanied by certain kinds of physical events, and it may sometimes appear that they influence each other or interact, but according to the theory this is an illusion, and the two realms actually operate quite independently of each other. Physical processes accompany mental experiences, but they do not cause them and are not caused by them. A thought cannot move a muscle, although the thought and the movement occur at the same time, and a pinprick does not cause the pain sensation that accompanies it. According to this doctrine, mind–body interaction is an illusion, similar to the illusion of the two clocks: if two clocks are standing side by side, their movements may *seem* to be linked by a kind of causal interaction, and they may even seem to be physically connected, but of course each clock moves quite independently. The suggestion is that minds and bodies do not really interact either; there is merely a psycho-physical parallelism between mental experiences and certain kinds of bodily processes.

Psycho-physical parallelism was more in harmony with scientific knowledge in the second half of the nineteenth century than any previous solution to the mind–body problem. Without violating the first law of thermodynamics, it explained how mental experiences seemed to cause physical events and vice versa. Once psychophysical parallelism became fashionable, the intellectual climate was favourable for the emergence of psychology as an independent discipline. Mental experiences were no longer downgraded to the level of trivial epiphenomena of brain processes but were considered to be worth studying in their own right. The pioneering experimental psychologists of the late nineteenth century were all psycho-physical parallelists, and it is doubtful that psychology would have emerged from the closet when it did had it not been for the popularity of the doctrine. The same may be said of the psychoanalytic theory of Sigmund Freud (1856–1939) that came to light at about the same time. Freud was also a psycho-physical parallelist who believed passionately that psychological phenomena have psychological causes. Epiphenomenalism, with its peculiar bias against mental experiences, or for that matter Descartes' brand of interactionism, could hardly have provided fertile soil for the germination of psychology or psychoanalysis.

In order to understand the subject matter and research methods of early experimental psychology, it is necessary to consider certain philosophical influences of a different kind. They emanated from nineteenth-century British philosophy, particularly the doctrines of associationism and empiricism. Both can be traced to the writings of the English empiricist philosopher John Locke (1632–1704).

Locke's *Essay Concerning Human Understanding* was published in 1690. Ten years later he added a chapter entitled "Of the Association of Ideas" to a revised edition of the book. This chapter outlined a theory of attraction between mental elements or ideas in terms that were reminiscent of Newton's gravitational theory, published in 1687, of attraction between physical bodies. Associationism was elaborated into a powerful theory by the early and mid-nineteenth-century philosophers James Mill (1773–1836) and his son John Stuart Mill (1806–1873). According to the Mills, mental experiences consist of elements of two kinds. Sensations are the elementary experiences (tastes, smells, sights, sounds, and feelings) that we have when our sense organs are stimulated, and ideas are the thoughts and images (memories) that we experience in the absence of sensory stimulation. Ideas have a tendency to become associated with one another, and complex ideas arise from the association of simple ideas. Once two ideas have become associated, they tend to call each other up, and it becomes difficult to experience one without the other. For example, the idea of redness is associated in most people's minds with warmth, so we tend to think of warmth whenever we think of redness. The association of ideas was supposed to explain the whole stream of consciousness that begins at birth and is interrupted only by dreamless sleep and death.

James Mill believed that a single law, later called the law of contiguity, was sufficient to explain all mental associations and complex ideas. According to this law, elements become associated when they are close to one another in time or space. Redness is associated with warmth because the two are often contiguous, as in a hearth full of glowing coals. John Stuart Mill complicated the theory by adding further laws of association, notably similarity (similar ideas tend to become associated) and frequency (the more frequently ideas occur together, the more strongly they become associated). He also abandoned his father's "mental mechanics" in favour of what he called "mental chemistry". As its name suggests, the idea was borrowed from chemistry, in which compounds often have properties that are quite different from the elements of which they are composed, a familiar example being water, the properties of which are not found in hydrogen or oxygen, the chemical constituents of water. John Stuart Mill argued that simple ideas combine to form complex ideas that are qualitatively different from their constituent elements, and that a complex idea may therefore not resemble the sum of its parts. For example, according to the law of contiguity, the idea of whiteness can arise from the association of several different colour sensations presented in rapid succession on a colour-mixing wheel, as Newton had demonstrated in his *Optiks*.

Associationist philosophy is reflected in the theories of the early experimental psychologists and psychoanalysts, and these will be discussed in more detail later in this chapter. John Stuart Mill's suggestion that mental wholes may be different from the sum of their parts became the central principle of the Gestalt school of psychology. Mental chemistry appeared in a different form in the theories of some of the early German experimental psychologists, although the leading German psychologist Wilhelm Wundt (1832–1920) was critical of British associationism. The structuralist school of the late nineteenth and early twentieth centuries drew heavily on associationist philosophy. The free association therapeutic technique of Sigmund Freud (1836–1939), and the word-association test of Carl Gustav Jung (1875–1961) – actually invented by the English explorer, amateur scientist, and psychologist Francis Galton (1822–1911) in 1883 – had their roots in associationist mental philosophy.

A late development in associationist philosophy that had far-reaching consequences in psychology was an idea put forward by the Scottish philosopher Alexander Bain (1818–1903). In Bain's version of associationism, the mental elements include sensations, ideas, emotions, and also elements of a radically different kind that no philosopher had previously taken into account, namely bodily movements. Bain distinguished between voluntary movements on the one hand and involuntary, automatic forms of behaviour on the other. He called the involuntary movements instincts, but most subsequent writers called them reflexes. Bain thought that both kinds of bodily movements could form associations with sensations, ideas, and emotions. It was only a short step from this to the later psychological theories of stimulus–response associations.

The concepts of stimulus and response are the building blocks of psychology of the behaviourist school, and they can be traced to the novel elements of Bain's associationism. The third and most important concept of behaviourism, the notion of the conditioned reflex, follows naturally from Bain's suggestion that bodily movements can form associations with other elements. Bain's influence on the early development of experimental psychology was enormous. It is worth pointing out that he was also the first person to dedicate his working life to mental philosophy, and in 1876 he founded the journal *Mind*, the first periodical in the world devoted to psychological questions.

Empiricism, an influential philosophical doctrine associated especially with the British empiricists John Locke (1632–1704), Bishop George Berkeley (1685–1753), and David Hume (1711–1776), held that all elements of knowledge, or in a less extreme version all factual knowledge as distinct from logically deduced inferences, are based on or derived from experience, and adherents to this view often took the experimental method as a prototype of knowledge acquisition in general. Locke believed that people are born with minds like blank slates on which their life experiences are later written. According to the empiricists, everything that we know is the result of information acquired through the senses and reflection on that information, and nothing is innate in the mind.

British empiricism had an important influence on the research methods of the early experimental psychologists. It encouraged them to tackle old questions that had previously been approached only by armchair speculation with new methods based on controlled observation. The doctrine that all knowledge comes ultimately from the senses led the empiricists to advocate a new rule of scientific method. It was this: reject as valueless all statements about the world that are not supported by evidence, and accept only those that can be verified by observation.

Private mental experiences, seen from the inside, so to speak, certainly counted as empirical evidence in nineteenth-century mental philosophy. It was even argued by some that introspective observations were more direct, and therefore more trustworthy, than observations of external events. The early experimental psychologists focused their attention mainly on mental experiences, and their research consisted largely of controlled introspection under experimental conditions. But a peculiar twist in the empiricist doctrine was later introduced by psychologists of the behaviourist school. They took the view that observations of another person's (or animal's) behaviour are "scientific", whereas observations of one's own mental processes are not. The behaviourists' anti-mentalistic view can be explained, at least in part, by the fact that they were trying to model psychology on older and more respected sciences, especially physics and biology, in which only publicly observable events are available as empirical evidence.

Biological roots

The Industrial Revolution, which transformed the social structures of northern Europe from the mid eighteenth century onwards, was accompanied by dramatic advances in many branches of natural philosophy, or what became known as natural science. Explanations based on miracles and magic gave way to a rationalistic world view that encouraged scientific research into the structure and function of living things, especially in England and France. Post-mortem dissections of human bodies, formerly frowned on by the Church, became acceptable, and the newly invented microscope enabled detailed investigations of nerve cells, muscles, and sense organs to be carried out. During the second half of the eigh-

teenth century physiology became established as a branch of science, and numerous investigations of reflexes and other bodily processes were published. Towards the end of the century the Italian physiologist Luigi Galvani (1737–1798) demonstrated that a frog's leg moves when a current of electricity is passed through it. This suggested that the nervous system is driven by electrical impulses, and from that basic insight the physiology of the nervous system was gradually unfolded.

By the 1820s knowledge of the nervous system had become quite sophisticated. In 1811 the Scottish anatomist Sir Charles Bell (1774–1842) discovered that there are two different kinds of nerves, those that carry information from the sense organs and enter the spinal cord from the back, and those that transmit impulses to the muscles and are attached to the front of the spinal cord. This important distinction between sensory (afferent) and motor (efferent) nerves was discovered independently in 1822 by the French physiologist François Magendie (1783–1855), and it became known as the Bell–Magendie law.

In 1861 and 1865 the French surgeon and anthropologist Paul Broca (1824–1880) reported the first scientific evidence linking a psychological function to a specific area of the brain. He described a series of patients with severe speech defects, but normal comprehension of spoken and written language, who had all suffered damage to an area of the cortex close to the left temple that was later called Broca's area. In 1874 the German neuropsychiatrist Karl Wernicke (1848–1905) discovered another brain area that was associated with language in a different way. Wernicke's area lies close to the left ear, and lesions in this region are accompanied by loss of *comprehension* of spoken and written language rather than any impairment of speech. Patients with lesions in Broca's or Wernicke's area hear non-verbal sounds, including music, normally. It says something about the pace of scientific advance that these areas were labelled "Constructiveness" and "Secretiveness" in Spurzheim's textbook of phrenology, published only a few decades earlier in 1834.

In 1850 the German physiologist Hermann von Helmholtz (1821–1894) published the first of a series of articles that were to play an important role in the later development of psychology. His early work was devoted to measuring the speed of nerve impulses. Nerve conduction had generally been assumed to be instantaneous, or at least as fast as light. Helmholtz showed empirically that it is in fact rather slow, about a million times slower than light. He later made important contributions to the physiology of vision and hearing. His teaching assistant for a time was Wilhelm Wundt (1832–1920), who was destined to identify psychology as an independent discipline in 1873 and to found the world's first psychological laboratory in Leipzig in 1879. The emphasis that Wundt and the other early experimental psychologists placed on the study of sensation and reaction time was partly due to the influence of Helmholtz. The development of reflexology in Russia and the emergence of the behaviourist school in the United States in the early twentieth century also owe a great deal to this physiological heritage, based as it was on reflex arcs.

A different kind of biological influence came from the theory of evolution. Evolutionary ideas were very much in vogue during the mid nineteenth century, and they gained enormous impetus from the publication in 1859 of *The Origin of Species by Means of Natural Selection, or the Preservation of Favoured Races in the Struggle for Life* by the English naturalist Charles Darwin (1809–1882). In spite of its rather off-putting title, the entire print run of 1250 copies was sold out on the day of publication. To explain the variety of life forms on earth, Darwin's theory offered a natural mechanism in place of theological speculation. The fundamental ideas are variation, heredity, and selection. There is variation among the individual members of a species, but offspring resemble their parents. The individuals that are best adapted to the environment produce more offspring than the others, and by this process of natural selection new species gradually evolve. The process that was later summed up as "the survival of the fittest" explained the great diversity of species in terms of evolution from a single (or perhaps a few) ancestors, and this provided an alternative to the book of Genesis.

Despite fierce opposition from the Church, Darwin's theory of evolution was rapidly accepted by the scientific community. The mechanistic assumptions underlying the theory harmonized with the style of thinking that had become fashionable during the Industrial Revolution. The theory appealed to Victorian readers also because it offered a natural model of the competitive economic system of capitalism that had recently developed. In the struggle for economic survival, as in nature, only the fittest survive.

Evolutionary ideas had an enormous impact on the early development of experimental psychology. First, it soon became apparent that empirical research is more fruitful than theological dogma and that animal behaviour may have some relevance to our understanding of human psychology. Human beings were viewed for the first time as members of the animal kingdom, although many people, excluding Darwin himself, inferred from the theory that the human species had reached a higher level of evolutionary development than other animals. It had previously been taken for granted that human beings are quite unlike other animals through their unique possession of rational souls, and Descartes believed that non-human animals are merely spongy machines. Second, individual differences between people, which had been neglected since ancient times, became a topic of serious enquiry once again. Because people considered themselves superior to other animals in intellectual capacity rather than strength or agility, early research into individual differences focused primarily on intelligence. Francis Galton (1822–1911), Darwin's half-cousin, devised the world's first intelligence test, founded and named the eugenics movement whose purpose was to improve the hereditary quality of the human race by selective breeding, and carried out the first statistical study of the inheritance of intelligence. In his book *Hereditary Genius*, published in 1869, he scrutinized the family trees of 415 distinguished judges, statesmen, military commanders, literary figures, scientists, poets, artists, and divines. He found that close relatives of these eminent people were often also eminent, but that distant relatives were not. For example, 48 per cent of their sons, 7 per cent of their grandsons, and only 1 per cent of their great-grandsons were eminent. Galton concluded from this that intelligence is largely hereditary. His influence can be traced in the history of British psychology through his disciple, the English statistician Karl Pearson

(1857–1936), and successive psychologists of the London school, including Charles Spearman (1863–1945), Sir Cyril Burt (1883–1971), and Hans Eysenck (1916–1997). The third and probably the most important way in which evolutionary ideas penetrated experimental psychology was in the form of an analogy. The early behaviourists interpreted learning as a process in which elements of behaviour that they called responses are selectively conditioned through association until eventually only the most successful responses survive and are strengthened. The process of learning was thought of as a kind of natural selection. Members of the functionalist school, for their part, interpreted virtually all behaviour from the point of view of its usefulness in the "struggle for life", as Darwin had called it. The influence of evolutionism is less apparent in the other major schools of psychology, which originated in non-English-speaking countries where Darwin's influence was not so strong.

The emergence of the discipline

The prevailing currents of philosophical and biological thinking converged towards the emergence of the new discipline of psychology in the second half of the nineteenth century. Mental philosophy, after a series of setbacks, was flourishing once again alongside natural philosophy. The desirability and feasibility of experimental investigations of behaviour and mental experience were becoming increasingly apparent through developments in the biological sciences. Philosophers and biologists had planted new ideas about sensation, association of ideas, reaction times, and reflexes, and these ideas looked ripe for the plucking.

Against this intellectual background, psychology finally emerged as an independent discipline in Germany in the 1880s. The experimental groundwork had been laid by the physiologist Ernst Heinrich Weber (1795–1878) and the philosopher and mystic Gustav Theodor Fechner (1801–1887), whose work I outlined in the answers to Questions 7 and 8 of the quiz in chapter 2. The date chosen by most historians for the birth of experimental psychology is 1879, the year in which Wilhelm Wundt (1832–1920) opened his laboratory in Leipzig. United States patriots sometimes make half-hearted attempts to dispute this, claiming that the first American psychologist, William James (1842–1910), opened a laboratory at Harvard University four years earlier. But the truth is that James was never very interested in experimental methods, and Wundt clearly has priority as the founder of experimental psychology because he alone was trying deliberately to create a new discipline. Within a decade experimental psychology was flourishing in several parts of Germany. Myths abound about the birth pangs of psychology, and it is worth pausing to consider exactly what happened, and what did not happen, in Germany in the 1880s. Attempts to understand mental experience and behaviour were nothing new. As we have seen, important contributions were made long before the time of Plato and Aristotle. Nor was the word *psychology* an invention of the nineteenth century. The Latin word *psychologia* emerged from obscure origins in Germany in the sixteenth century, but no one is certain who coined it or exactly when it was first used. The English word *psychology* first appeared in 1693 in Steven Blankaart's *The Physical Dictionary: Wherein the terms of Anatomy, the names and causes of Diseases, chyrugical Instruments and their Use; are accurately Describ'd*. Blankaart refers to "*Anthropologia*, the Description of Man, or the Doctrin concerning him [which is divided] into Two Parts; viz. *Anatomy*, which treats of the Body, and *Psychology*, which treats of the Soul". The word *psychology* was used sporadically throughout the eighteenth and early nineteenth centuries, but it was not until the 1830s that it began to be used frequently and came to be widely understood. Not even the use of experimental methods for investigating psychological questions were new to the German experimental psychologists. Experiments had been applied to psychological problems during the earlier part of the nineteenth century by philosophers such as Fechner, biologists such as Helmholtz, physicians such as Magendie, and amateurs such as Galton, as I have described. So what was new in Germany in the 1880s?

Two historical developments distinguished early German experimental psychology from all that went before. The first was an attempt to separate psychology from the other biological sciences and from philosophy, and the second was the formation of a self-conscious and organized community of professional psychologists. Wundt was in the vanguard of the first of these movements but strongly opposed to the second.

The opening sentence of Wundt's *Principles of Physiological Psychology*, the first major textbook, published in 1873, of what he later called experimental psychology, reads: "The book that I herewith offer to the public attempts to mark out a new domain of science." He was well aware that experimental psychology of great importance had already been published. In Leipzig, where he was soon to settle, the physiologist Ernst Heinrich Weber (1795–1878) and the philosopher-mystic Gustav Theodor Fechner (1801–1887) had already done ground-breaking experimental work. Their most important works, published in 1846 and 1860 respectively, established fundamental laws relating the physical intensity of stimuli to the psychological magnitude of sensations and opened up an area of psychological research that is still called psychophysics. But Weber regarded psychophysics as a branch of physiology and Fechner regarded it as a branch of philosophy. Wundt was the first to recognize experimental psychology as a "new domain of science".

The emergence of psychology as an independent discipline led to attempts by some of the younger German psychologists to establish an organized professional community. Wundt was vigorously opposed to this, and the German Psychological Association was unable to meet in Leipzig until after his death. The professionalization of psychology in Germany was not nearly as rapid or as thorough as in the United States, where its philosophical roots were shallower. Starting with the laboratory at Harvard University set up by William James in 1875, psychological research centres sprang up all over the United States in the late nineteenth and early twentieth centuries, and United States psychologists were quickly organized into a powerful professional association. The bulk of psychological research and publication none the less remained centred in Germany, and German psychology flourished until the rise of the Nazi dictatorship in the 1930s drove many of its leading lights abroad.

The development of psychology in France and Britain, the natural cradles of psychology from a historical point of view, was considerably slower. In France, the materialist and anti-psychological bias that arose during the Enlightenment was never completely eradicated, and it retarded the development of psychology in all areas except physiological and medical psychology. In addition, the rationalist approach to mental philosophy introduced by Descartes engendered a certain resistance to empirical methods in France. In Britain, the conservative and ecclesiastical educational policies of the old universities of Oxford and Cambridge created an atmosphere hostile to new trends in both the humanities and the sciences. Many of the greatest scientists of the nineteenth century, including

Darwin and Galton, were amateurs of independent means who worked outside the framework of the university system. In 1877 the Senate of Cambridge University turned down a proposal from the philosopher James Ward (1843–1925) to establish a psychological laboratory on the grounds that it would "insult religion by putting the human soul in a pair of  scales". At Oxford University, experimental psychology was not officially taught until 1936. Even the new University of London, founded in 1836, was distinctly conservative in its administrative and scientific attitudes. For example, in 1837 John Elliotson (1791–1868), the university's first professor of medicine, began hypnotizing patients in an attempt to find a new treatment for certain nervous complaints. His methods were criticized in the influential medical journal *The Lancet*, and the University Council passed a resolution forbidding "the practice of mesmerism or animal magnetism within the Hospital". In 1842 a surgeon performed a leg amputation on a hypnotized patient who apparently felt no pain during the operation, but when he reported the case to the Royal Medical and Chirugical Society, the record of his paper was struck from the minutes on the grounds that surgery without pain is immoral and that "patients ought to suffer pain while their surgeons are operating". It is hardly surprising that psychology was slow to penetrate the conservative academic and scientific establishment in Britain.

The era of schools

From the end of the nineteenth century until the 1930s, psychology was fragmented into several more or less independent schools that were at loggerheads with one another on theoretical issues, research methods, and the kinds of psychological processes that they considered worthy of study. Structuralism and functionalism sprang out of the philosophical and biological antecedents of psychology – associationist philosophy and evolutionary theory respectively. Behaviourism and Gestalt psychology arose initially as revolts against the other schools. Psychoanalysis developed independently outside the academic establishment. By the end of the Second World War the schools had declined, although psychoanalysis continued to thrive as an organized profession outside the mainstream of academic psychology, and a modified form of neobehaviourism remained influential. But long after the decline of the schools, current areas of psychological research retain unmistakable traces of their historical origins.

Structuralism   The structuralist school of psychology was based chiefly on Wundt's *Outlines of Psychology*, published in Germany in 1897, and Edward Bradford Titchener's *An Outline of Psychology*, published in the United States in 1896. Titchener (1867–1927) was born in England, and after studying philosophy at Oxford he worked for a short time in Wundt's laboratory in Leipzig. In 1895 he became a professor of psychology at Cornell University in New York, where he attracted a considerable following.

The structuralists studied mental experience by analysing its elements, their properties, and the way they combined with one another. The most important elements were sensations, but attention was also paid to ideas (images of imagination and memory) and feelings. The chief method of investigation was introspection – people's observation of their own mental processes under rigorously controlled experimental conditions. Wundt restricted his experimental work to simple mental elements. Complex thought processes, including all those involving language, he classified as social psychology and investigated by non-experimental methods, particularly by examining their products in primitive cultures. Titchener, and also younger German psychologists such as Oswald Külpe (1862–1915) and Hermann von Ebbinghaus (1850–1909), repudiated this distinction and brought higher mental processes into the ambit of experimental psychology. For example, Ebbinghaus pioneered the experimental study of verbal memory in the 1880s.

Structuralism went into decline in Germany with the advent of Nazism in the 1930s and disappeared from psychology in the United States shortly after Titchener's death in 1927. Current research on sensation, especially in the area of psychophysics, is none the less strongly coloured by its structuralist heritage.

Functionalism   The functionalist school was launched in 1896 in an article by the United States pragmatist philosopher and psychologist John Dewey (1859–1952). It flourished for a considerable time at the University of Chicago under the influence of Dewey, George Herbert Mead (1863–1931), and others, and at Columbia University, where Edward Thorndike (1874–1949) and Robert Woodworth (1869–1962) were its most influential champions. It represented a deliberate attempt to introduce evolutionary ideas into psychology. Instead of trying to unravel the structure of mental experience, the functionalists investigated mental experience and especially behaviour from the standpoint of their functional value in adapting the organism to its environment. They put forward the novel idea that conscious experiences arise in situations where automatic, reflex behaviour is inadequate to meet the needs of the organism. For example, a person who is learning to ride a bicycle is at first conscious of every movement, but as the skill develops the behaviour gradually becomes automatic, and conscious control eventually disappears altogether when it is no longer needed. According to the functionalists, consciousness evolved to serve the kind of instrumental function involved in learning to ride a bicycle. The functionalists, true to their evolutionary origins, were the first psychologists to use non-human animals in experiments. For example, Thorndike invented a puzzle box for investigating problem solving in cats and dogs.

During the 1920s and 1930s, functionalism was gradually swallowed up by that younger and more radical school of behaviourism that was gaining ground at that time. Current research on thinking and problem solving owes something to its functionalist pioneers, but the most important legacies of functionalism are probably sociobiology and the use of animals in psychological research.

Behaviourism In 1913 the United States psychologist John B(roadus) Watson (1878–1958) broke away from the functionalist school in an article that shocked the psychological establishment in the United States and launched the behaviourist school. In the succeeding decades behaviourism became an enormously powerful force in United States psychology, although it was never as influential in other countries. Watson declared the theoretical goal of psychology to be "the prediction and control of behavior". This represented a ˙complete break with the classical experimental psychology of the structuralists, which involved neither prediction nor control nor behaviour.

Watson considered the introspective methods of the structuralists and functionalists to be unscientific, and he excluded everything except behaviour from psychology. Mental processes like thinking were to be regarded as nothing more than small-scale movements of the vocal apparatus, and emotion was nothing but the secretion of glands, in other words, thinking and feeling were both reinterpreted as special kinds of behaviour. Watson borrowed the doctrine of operationalism from positivist philosophy and defined the meaning of psychological concepts to be literally the operations through which they are measured – for example, according to a strict operational definition, intelligence is what intelligence tests measure, nothing more and nothing less.

According to the behaviourists, virtually all behaviour can be explained as the product of learning, and all learning consists of the formation of conditioned reflexes. These are simple associations between stimuli that excite the sense organs and responses that were defined as muscular or glandular reactions to stimuli. Watson was probably not aware of the work of the Russian reflexologists when he developed his theory. But the famous experiments on classical conditioning conducted by Ivan Petrovich Pavlov (1849–1936), in which hungry dogs learned to salivate to an initially neutral stimulus such as the sound of a bell by repeated pairing of the sound with food, added further impetus to the behaviourist movement when they became known in the United States.

The most influential proponent of neo-behaviourism since the 1940s was the United States psychologist B(urrhus) F(rederic) Skinner (1904–1990), who initiated the study of instrumental or operant conditioning, a learning process whereby the relative frequency of a response increases as a result of reward that is contingent on the response being emitted. As complete explanations of all forms of behaviour, the doctrines of classical and instrumental conditioning have lost much of their force in the face of mounting attacks from various sources and the decline of positivist dogmas, but neo-behaviourism is still an influential psychological theory in the English-speaking world. Current theorizing and research on learning are based very largely on neo-behaviourist ideas and methods, and instrumental conditioning plays an important part in several areas of applied psychology.

Gestalt psychology   The Gestalt school (from the German *Gestalt* shape, form, or whole; there is no adequate English translation) emerged in 1912 with the publication of an article on apparent movement by the German psychologist Max Wertheimer

(1880–1943). Wertheimer discussed a class of visual illusions that arise when two visual stimuli a few centimetres apart are displayed in an alternating sequence, and he identified a number of stages (*Stadien*). With an interval between the stimuli shorter than about 25 milliseconds the stimuli, though possibly flickering, appear to be simultaneous, and with an interstimulus interval over about 400 milliseconds there is no illusion and the stimuli are seen to alternate, but between about 25 and 400 milliseconds, powerful illusions of movement are created, including phi movement, a form of pure objectless apparent movement without the appearance of any entity actually moving, occurring under certain precisely specified conditions. The various phenomena of apparent movement underlie the effects created by illuminated signboards with arrows or other elements that appear to move, and they also explain the motion pictures of cinema and television.

The significance of phi movement is that it provides a vivid example of a mental experience that cannot be explained in terms of elementary sensations, because the whole (Gestalt) is different from the sum of its parts. The Gestalt psychologists, particularly Wertheimer and the other founding German Gestaltists Kurt Koffka (1886–1941), Wolfgang Köhler (1887–1967), and Kurt Lewin (1890–1947), objected strenuously to the analytical approach of the structuralists. Mental experience, they thought, will never be understood by analysing its elements. They were influenced by the work of the Austrian physicist, philosopher, and psychologist Ernst Mach (1838–1916) on electromagnetic fields. One of the striking features of force fields in physics is that they cannot be broken down into elements but are, so to speak, irreducible wholes. The Gestalt psychologists believed that to understand mental experience it is not the elementary sensations that must be studied, but the relations between them.

A classic example used by the Gestalt psychologists is melodic constancy. The sequence of notes C, D, E, C, C, D, E, C played evenly on any musical instrument is instantly recognizable as the well-known folk tune *Frère Jacques*. The sequence F, G, A, F, F, G, A, F, which does not contain a single element in common with the first, sounds like the same tune. But the sequence E, D, C, C, E, D, C, C, which contains the same elements as the first sequence in a new configuration, sounds like *Three Blind Mice*, an entirely different Gestalt. The point of all this, according to the Gestalt psychologists, is that an analytic investigation of the elements of consciousness cannot reveal the important facts of mental experience. To understand the mind, we must study overall patterns, configurations, or wholes. The influence of Gestalt ideas in Germany and Austria receded with the rise of Nazism. Wertheimer, Koffka, Köhler, and Lewin emigrated to the United States in the 1920s and 1930s, by which time behaviourism, a virulent strain of elementalism, had gained a strong foothold there. But in the field of perception Gestalt ideas turned out to be indispensable, and contemporary research into perception in general and perceptual illusions in particular retains a distinctly Gestalt flavour.

Psychoanalysis The fundamental ideas of the psychoanalytic school, which grew up from the 1890s onwards around the Austrian psychiatrist Sigmund Freud (1856–1939), were outlined in chapter 1. It is necessary here to add only a few words about the social origins of this school that distinguish it from the others. Wundt and Titchener, Dewey, Thorndike, and the other functionalists, Watson and Skinner, Wertheimer, Koffka, Köhler, and Lewin were all academic psychologists. The goal that they all shared in common was to understand – or as Watson and Skinner would have it, to predict and control – psychological processes. Freud, on the other hand, was a physician whose psychoanalytic couch was visited by a stream of neurotic clients urgently in need of treatment. His primary goal was to find a way of relieving their crippling neuroses. His therapeutic methods were far removed from the research techniques of the academic laboratories, and his theories were not designed to be tested experimentally. His successors, including the Swiss psychologist Carl Gustav Jung (1875–1961) and the Austrian psychoanalysts Alfred Adler (1870–1937) and Melanie Klein (1882–1960), were also primarily clinicians rather than researchers.

The psychoanalytic school, although it grew into a large, powerful, and well-organized movement, never gained a foothold in the citadels of academic psychology, although the indirect influence of Freud's brilliantly original ideas on psychological theory is incalculable. In view of its social origins, it is hardly surprising that the influence of psychoanalysis is most strongly evident in the areas of abnormal psychology, emotion, and motivation.

Further reading

The account of Psammetichus's experiment discussed in the text was reported in part 1, book 2, paragraph 2 of Herodotus's *The histories* (translated by A. de Sélincourt, Harmondsworth: Penguin, 1972, original work completed *circa* 429 BC). The standard history of psychology is Edwin G. Boring's *A history of experimental psychology* (2nd ed., New York: Appleton-Century-Crofts, 1957). It is a useful and readable book, but it focuses on Great Men and "Zeitgeists" rather than the evolution of ideas, and its reliability has been questioned, especially in its treatment of Wundt. Other popular historical texts are Leslie Hearnshaw's *The shaping of modern psychology: An historical introduction* (London: Routledge & Kegan Paul, 1987) and David Hothersall's *History of psychology* (3rd ed., New York: McGraw-Hill, 1995). Richard L. Gregory's *Mind in science: A history of explanations in psychology and physics* (Harmondsworth: Penguin, 1984) deals with selected topics but is highly recommendable.

A brilliant and fascinating account of the evolution of hypnosis and psychoanalysis is Henri F. Ellenberger's *The discovery of the unconscious: The history and evolution of dynamic psychiatry* (New York: Basic Books, 1970). For information on early German experimental psychology, see Robert W. Rieber (Ed.), *Wilhelm Wundt and the making of a scientific psychology* (New York: Plenum, 1980).

The best way of learning about the history of psychology is by reading the original texts. Rieber's book on Wundt contains translations of some of Wundt's original writings. A number of volumes containing selections from other historically important psychological texts are available. The best of these are edited by Ludy T. Benjamin (Ed.), *A history of psychology: Original sources and contemporary research* (2nd ed., New York: McGraw-Hill, 1997); James F. Brennan (Ed.), *Readings in the history and systems of psychology* (2nd ed., Upper Saddle River, NJ: Prentice Hall, 1998); Richard J. Herrnstein and Edwin G. Boring (Eds), *A source book in the history of psychology* (Cambridge, MA: Harvard University Press, 1965); Thomas H. Leahy (Ed.), *A history of psychology: Main currents in psychological thought* (4th ed., Upper Saddle River, NJ: Prentice Hall, 1997); and Robert I. Watson (Ed.), *Basic writings in the history of psychology* (New York: Oxford University Press, 1979).

Chapter 6

Psychology as a profession

This chapter is about applied psychology and the various professions and careers that are open to psychologists. Before the Second World War, virtually all psychologists were employed as teachers and researchers in universities and colleges, and psychology was practised almost exclusively as an academic discipline. Since the 1950s, several fields of applied psychology have emerged, and a wider range of careers is now available to psychology graduates than to graduates of almost any other subject.

Psychologists work in a wide range of settings, including universities and colleges, hospitals, clinics, counselling agencies, research establishments, schools, prisons, government departments, and commercial and industrial companies. An increasing number of psychologists are self-employed in private practice. The major branches of professional psychology that are open only to properly qualified psychologists are psychological teaching and research, clinical and counselling psychology, educational and school psychology, occupational and industrial/organizational psychology, and forensic and criminological psychology. Careers in these professions generally require postgraduate qualifications in addition to a good first degree in psychology, and competition for places on the training courses is generally intense. In the United Kingdom, a good first degree usually means first class or upper second class. In the United States it is measured by the grade-point average (GPA) of the degree, and entry to most graduate programmes in psychology are based also on good performance on the multiple-choice Graduate Record Exam (GRE).

It has been estimated that only 15–20 per cent of psychology graduates in the United Kingdom become professional psychologists. Of those approximately one-third work in the public sector for the National Health Service, the Civil Service, and the armed forces, one-third work in industry and commerce, and one-tenth teach psychology in schools, colleges, and universities. However, the line between psychological and non-psychological professions is rather blurred, and a number of professions such as market research and psychotherapy welcome psychologists but are open to graduates in other subjects as well. In addition, there are several professions allied to psychology, such as social work, speech therapy, and school-teaching, in which psychologists are often employed. I pointed out in chapter 3 that many of the literacy, numeracy, interpersonal, technical, and practical skills that are learnt as part of an education in psychology are useful in many different fields of employment.

The world's largest association of psychologists, the American Psychological Association (APA), was founded in 1892 and by the late 1990s had a membership of more than 155,000 psychologists and students. The second largest, The British Psychological Society (BPS), was founded in 1901 and incorporated by Royal Charter in 1965 and has about 25,000 members. In some countries, steps have been taken to discourage the practice of psychology and pseudo-psychology by unqualified people. In Britain, the BPS has been authorized since 1987 to maintain a voluntary Register of Chartered Psychologists. Only those on the register are legally entitled to call themselves chartered psychologists, to use the letters C.Psychol. after their names, and to receive practising certificates. In the United States, most state legislatures have introduced much stronger licensing laws that define certain psychological services and make it illegal for unqualified people to offer these services for payment. The requirements vary from state to sate but typically include a doctoral degree in psychology, a year's supervised work during graduate study, a year's post-doctoral supervision, and a pass in the state licensing examination. Licensing laws are rare in other parts of the world, but some form of legal registration at least as strong as the British system operates in most European countries, and also in Australia, New Zealand, South Africa, and Japan.

It is obviously impossible, in a short chapter such as this, to deal comprehensively with all occupations open to psychologists. I shall restrict my comments mainly to the major professions and try to convey a realistic picture of what is involved in each of them. I shall outline the qualifications and training necessary for the major careers in psychology and offer some practical advice for people who are thinking about studying the subject.

Psychology teaching and research

Teaching posts in psychology exist in most universities and colleges, and there are also posts for psychology teaching in adult education centres, schools, and other teaching establishments. In the United Kingdom, research posts are available in universities, the Civil Service, trade unions, commercial and voluntary organizations, and specialized research establishments.

Psychologists teaching at degree level are expected to concentrate mainly or solely on their own areas of specialization. For example, a developmental psychologist is not normally required to teach sensation and perception, or any other topic far removed from developmental psychology, except perhaps at an elementary level. Psychology teachers in schools and colleges are usually expected to teach a much wider range of topics. For example, a schoolteacher in the United Kingdom preparing candidates for A level examinations in psychology is likely to have to cover the whole syllabus.

Teaching, in one form or another, takes up a large proportion of the working time of most university psychologists, and an even larger proportion of the working time of those in other institutions of higher education. One of the most common methods of teaching in higher education is lecturing to large groups of students. Most lecturers use fairly detailed notes that they keep up to date by consulting books, journal articles, and Internet sites and by attending conferences and workshops at which researchers discuss their latest findings. Other commonly used teaching methods are seminars with medium-sized groups of students and tutorials with

individuals or small groups of students. Psychologists teaching in universities are often involved in running laboratory classes and supervising the research projects of final-year undergraduates and the theses or dissertations of postgraduate research students up to the doctoral (Ph.D., D.Phil., or Psy.D.) level. Research supervision is usually done on a one-to-one basis.

In addition to their teaching duties, and various administrative tasks connected with the running of their departments, university psychologists are required by their contracts of employment to carry out and publish research. Non-university psychology teachers are not generally required to do research, and most (though by no means all) of the psychological research published in the leading journals comes from university departments. It is not essential to be in a university department, or for that matter to have a job at all, in order to carry out research. In theory, anybody can do it, but psychology departments are ideal environments for research because of the technical facilities and access to specialist information and resources that they provide.

In order to carry out original research, a psychologist must first become familiar with the work that has already been done by others in the chosen area of investigation. A familiarity with the "state of the art" in a particular research area may reveal certain unanswered questions. A leap of imagination and a measure of good luck are needed to choose a line of investigation that is likely to prove fruitful and to design an appropriate research method. Very often, the research cannot be carried out without financial support from a research funding body that has first to be convinced that the research is worth doing. Competition for research funding is intense, and most applications fail. If funding is obtained and the research works out successfully, then the investigators (research projects are usually collaborative efforts) may decide to submit their results to an appropriate journal. The manuscript will then be read by referees chosen by the journal's editor, in the light of which the editor will accept it for publication, reject it, or send it back to the authors for revision. Many of the best psychological journals reject over 80 per cent of the manuscripts that are submitted to them.

Teaching and research do not suit all temperaments. Psychology is a rapidly changing subject, and continuous effort is needed to keep abreast of new developments. Many university psychologists find it difficult to strike the right balance between teaching and research, and between reading and writing. On the other hand, the relatively informal working conditions of universities and the freedom (within limits) to pursue one's own interests are attractive to some people. Applicants for teaching and research posts are usually judged mainly by their formal qualifications, publications, and experience. Conditions of supply and demand are constantly in flux, but in general the best teaching and research jobs are extremely hard to get. For university posts, a good first degree in psychology, a higher degree, and a record of research and publication are usually needed. Psychology teachers in schools and further education colleges are generally required to hold recognized teaching qualifications. A Diploma in the Applied Psychology of Teaching was introduced in the United Kingdom in 1991.

Clinical and counselling psychology

Clinical psychologists assess and treat people with mental disorders. They work in hospitals and clinics, health centres, and private practice. In the United Kingdom, most clinical psychologists are employed by the National Health Service in psychiatric and general hospitals. Others work in general practitioners' health centres or in specialist clinics, and some are in private practice. Clinical psychologists usually work in collaboration with psychiatrists, medical practitioners, social workers, nurses, and in some cases educational or school psychologists. Counselling psychologists use most of the same methods as clinical psychologists, but their clients tend to be people with adjustment problems rather than mental disorders. Counselling psychologists help people to resolve crises, solve problems, make decisions, and improve the quality of their lives. They work with individuals, couples, and families in a variety of settings, including counselling agencies, general practitioners' surgeries, educational establishments, business organizations, and private practice. Both clinical and counselling psychology are based largely on research in abnormal psychology (see chapter 3).

One important part of the work of clinical and counselling psychologists is psychological assessment. When a psychologist sees a client for the first time, the initial task is generally to try to understand the client's problem. This usually involves detailed interviews covering matters directly and indirectly related to the presenting problem. During these initial interviews, the psychologist may take a case history, paying close attention to what the client says, to things the client conspicuously avoids saying, and to various aspects of the client's non-verbal behaviour that might provide further insights into the problem. It often becomes apparent early on that the presenting problem disguises a different underlying problem. For example, the client may complain about being unable to sleep, but it may transpire that the underlying problem is depression and insomnia is merely a symptom.

Clinical and counselling psychologists sometimes use psychometric tests in their assessment of clients. The best of these are tests that have been carefully standardized on large samples from psychiatric and non-psychiatric populations to establish norms and to ensure reliability and validity. Psychometric tests can be especially helpful in answering questions such as the following: Is there any evidence of brain damage in this man? What is the nature of this woman's disorder? Does this child meet the diagnostic criteria for autistic disorder? Other sources of information used by clinical and counselling psychologists in assessments of clients include reports from relatives, nurses, general practitioners, and other people acquainted with the client, and diaries that the client may be asked to keep. A psychologist's assessment is often only one contribution from a team in which several medical and paramedical professions may be represented.

Perhaps the most important part of a clinical psychologist's work is the treatment of mental disorders. The major therapeutic methods can be divided, rather arbitrarily and with some overlap, into three categories: verbal psychotherapy, behaviour modification, and group therapy. Counselling techniques are generally based on the same methods.

Verbal psychotherapy includes several techniques of dealing with clients' problems through talking. Among the most prominent verbal techniques are the psychoanalytic therapies based on the writings of the Austrian physician Sigmund Freud (1856–1939) and his followers. Between 10 and 20 per cent of United States clinical psychologists use predominantly psychoanalytic techniques, and the proportion is much smaller in the United Kingdom. The most distinctive characteristic of these types of therapy is the attempt that is made to interpret unconscious sources of psychological problems. The basic techniques of psychoanalytic therapy were outlined in chapter 1.

A popular technique of counselling and verbal psychotherapy is client-centred therapy, based on the work of the United States psychologist Carl Rogers (1902–1987). Unlike their psychoanalytic colleagues, client-centred counsellors and therapists deliberately refrain from interpreting what their clients say, and they do not probe, advise, suggest, or persuade. Their approach is therefore sometimes called non-directive counselling or non-directive therapy. The fundamental assumption behind this approach is that people are capable of identifying the sources of their own emotional problems and of working out solutions for themselves once they are freed from feelings of anxiety and insecurity. To encourage this, the counsellor or therapist tries to establish genuine empathy with the client and to convey an attitude of "unconditional positive regard" in the context of a permissive, accepting, non-threatening relationship in which the client can come to grips with the problem without fear. The therapist helps by clarifying, rephrasing, and reflecting back the feelings or emotions that lie behind the client's remarks. For example, if a client says "This is just a waste of time, and I'm just as depressed as I was last week", a client-centred counsellor or therapist might reply: "You feel frustrated and angry because the sessions don't seem to be helping your depression". Comments of that kind are supposed to help the client to see things more clearly.

A technique of verbal psychotherapy based on a fundamentally different set of assumptions is cognitive therapy. It is aimed at modifying people's beliefs, expectancies, assumptions, and styles of thinking, on the assumption that psychological problems often stem from erroneous patterns of thinking and distorted perceptions of reality that can be identified and corrected. It has been applied especially to the treatment of depression. One form of cognitive therapy is rational–emotive therapy, pioneered by the United States psychologist Albert Ellis (born 1913). Rational–emotive therapists believe that mental disorders are caused by the ways in which people interpret events in their lives, rather than by the events themselves, and that it is only when these interpretations are irrational that mental disorders arise. For example, people who are rejected in love may (quite rationally) believe that they are unfortunate or unlucky, in which case feelings of regret, frustration, or irritation may arise. But if they (irrationally) interpret the rejection as proof that they are worthless, unlovable, or even hateful human beings, then feelings of extreme anxiety or depression may develop, and neuroses may begin to emerge. Rational–emotive therapists therefore challenge the irrational aspects of their clients' belief systems in an openly directive manner. They try to persuade their clients to adopt more rational beliefs, and to achieve this they use suggestion, argument, and many specialized techniques developed by Ellis and his followers.

The methods of behaviour modification are based on the fundamental assumptions that most mental disorders can be interpreted as maladaptive patterns of behaviour, that these patterns result from learning processes, and that the appropriate methods of treatment involve the unlearning of these behaviour patterns and the learning of new ones. Psychologists who practise behaviour modification or behaviour therapy believe that to eliminate the symptoms of a mental disorder is to eliminate the disorder, and they reject the notion of hidden causes underlying psychoanalytic theories in particular. The behavioural approach to causes and cures has its roots in the work of the United States psychologist John Broadus Watson (1878–1958), the founder of behaviourism (see chapter 5).

A behaviour modification technique that is held to be extremely effective in the treatment of phobias is called systematic desensitization. A phobia is a persistent, irrational fear of some object, activity, or situation called a phobic stimulus, resulting in a compelling desire to avoid it. The presence or anticipation of the phobic stimulus triggers anxiety or a panic attack, although the person acknowledges the fear to be irrational, and the phobic stimulus is either avoided or endured with dread. Among the most common are agoraphobia (open spaces), arachnophobia (spiders), claustrophobia (confined spaces), nosophobia (illness), ophidiophobia (snakes), and thanatophobia (death); less well-known and more exotic examples are ergophobia (working), phobophobia (acquiring a phobia), triskaidekaphobia (the number 13), and deipnophobia (dinner-parties or dining). Systematic desensitization is a behavioural treatment for phobias and other disorders developed in the 1950s by the South African psychiatrist Joseph Wolpe (1915–1997). It is a counter-conditioning technique in which the phobic stimulus (spiders, say) is repeatedly paired with a response that is physiologically incompatible with fear and anxiety, such as deep muscular relaxation. The therapist first helps the client to draw up a hierarchy of increasingly anxiety-provoking imaginary situations involving the phobic stimulus. The hierarchy may range from (1) "My daughter shows me a drawing she has made of a spider's web" to (10) "I wake up in the middle of the night to find a large, hairy spider crawling slowly over my face". Next, the therapist

teaches the client to enter a state of deep muscular relaxation. Up to half a dozen therapeutic sessions may be devoted to hierarchy construction and relaxation training before the therapy proper begins. During this final phase, the client enters a relaxed state and visualizes the lowest item in the hierarchy as vividly as possible without tensing up. At the slightest feeling of tension or anxiety, the client raises a finger and is instructed by the therapist to stop thinking about the phobic stimulus until deep relaxation is restored. When the client can repeatedly visualize the lowest item in the hierarchy without tension or anxiety, the second item is attempted. With the therapist's assistance, the client works slowly up the hierarchy until the most anxiety-provoking item has been conquered. The evidence suggests that the effects of systematic desensitization often transfer to situations in which the real phobic stimulus, rather than just an imagined image of it, is encountered, although there is considerable controversy over how and why the technique works.

A different technique of behaviour modification is based on the principles of instrumental or operant conditioning worked out by the United States psychologist Burrhus F. Skinner (1904–1990) and outlined in the answer to Question 14 of the quiz in chapter 2. It is most often used to treat people with learning disabilities, communication disorders, autistic disorder, and severe mental disorders such as schizophrenia. This therapeutic technique is essentially a method of training through reinforcement or reward. For example, a child with severe expressive language disorder may be exposed to training sessions during which the therapist shapes the child's verbal behaviour by rewarding – with hugs, encouraging noises, or chocolates – successive approximations to recognizable speech sounds, then words, then phrases, then finally sentences. In hospital wards for people with schizophrenia, "token economies" are sometimes established. In a token economy, the patients' access to privileges such as special foods, cigarettes, or television sets is made contingent on their performance of certain target behaviour patterns, such as dressing or speaking normally or interacting with other patients on the ward. To get the rewards, a patient has to accumulate a certain number of tokens, which are given out by the ward staff whenever they observe target behaviour patterns. Token economies have been shown to work, in so far as they produce dramatic increases in target behaviour patterns, but some psychologists consider them objectionable on account of their gross manipulativeness.

Cognitive behaviour modification is a form of verbal psychotherapy based on a mixture of cognitive therapy and behaviour modification in which the client or patient learns to replace dysfunctional self-speech (such as *I knew I'd never be able to cope with this job*) with adaptive alternatives (*The job's not going well, but I am capable of working out a plan to overcome the problems*). Its applications include anger control, stress management, coping with anxiety, and developing social skills.

The last category of therapeutic techniques includes various forms of group therapy. These techniques range from traditional group therapies, adapted from techniques originally intended for individual counselling or therapy, to more recent encounter, sensitivity, marathon, growth, confrontation, and Gestalt group therapies, whose aims and methods are somewhat different. It is impossible to give an adequate summary of these techniques here, but the central idea underlying many of them can be stated simply. If a group of people meet regularly under the guidance of a therapist, and if the group members are encouraged to relate to one another in an open and forthright manner, then feelings of isolation may give way to a sense of mutual emotional support, the group members may benefit by seeing their problems in a new perspective created by an awareness of the problems of others, and feedback from other group members may help them to understand themselves better, and teach them how to express their feelings and how to trust other people. Many of the popular group therapies involve interpersonal games and activities calculated to foster trust, self-awareness, and social sensitivity. The more radical group therapies lie partly outside the mainstream of clinical and counselling psychology and are often regarded with suspicion by professionals because there is no convincing evidence that they work.

To become a Chartered Clinical Psychologist in the United Kingdom, you need a first degree in psychology accredited by the BPS, followed by an accredited diploma or Master's degree in clinical psychology. This takes an extra two or three years. Competition for places on postgraduate clinical psychology training courses is severe, and a good first degree and some relevant work experience are usually required for the applicant to stand a realistic chance of gaining a place. To become a counselling psychologist you need a first degree in psychology accredited by the BPS followed by a Diploma in Counselling Psychology or a BPS-accredited postgraduate qualification.

Educational and school psychology

In the United States, educational and school psychologists are normally trained in departments of education rather than psychology, and after graduating, educational psychologists are employed in colleges and universities and school psychologists are employed in schools. In the United Kingdom this distinction does not exist, and educational psychologists are school psychologists. They are employed by local authorities, and they work chiefly in child guidance clinics and school psychological services, but a growing number work as independent or private consultants. There are also posts for educational psychologists in assessment centres, community schools, and children's hospitals. Educational and school psychology rely to some extent on research in abnormal and developmental psychology (see chapter 3).

Educational or school psychologists are trained in both education and psychology, and their work involves the diagnosis and treatment of educational, emotional, and behavioural problems in children of all ages up to the late teens. They deal with children who have problems such as visual and hearing handicaps, learning difficulties, specific disabilities in the areas of reading and arithmetic, emotional problems including examination anxiety, social and personality problems, school phobia and truancy, language difficulties, and problems arising from child abuse. They work closely with teachers and parents, often as members of multi-disciplinary teams that include general practitioners, psychiatrists, and social workers. In the United Kingdom they have certain statutory responsibilities connected with the assessment of children with special educational needs. Children are referred to educational psychologists chiefly by schoolteachers or parents, often because of poor scholastic performance, educational underachievement, or disruptive or withdrawn behaviour in school or at home.

One of the main functions of educational psychologists is

psychological assessment and diagnosis. For example, if a child is performing badly at school, an educational psychologist may be asked to offer an expert opinion as to whether this is due to lack of ability, emotional disturbance, social or interpersonal problems with teachers or other children, difficulties in the home environment, some form of mental disorder, or simply poor eyesight or hearing. The child's parents and teachers are likely to have views of their own about the source of the problem, and the child may also offer an explanation, but the root cause may turn out, on careful investigation, to be something quite different. In carrying out assessment and diagnosis, educational or school psychologists use interviews and psychometric tests specifically designed to provide answers to questions of this kind. Other sources of information include school records and interviews with teachers, parents, and social workers. In some cases educational psychologists make home visits to observe children in their family environments.

Apart from assessment and diagnosis, educational psychologists are also involved in the treatment of children with problems. The treatment may be direct, as in individual or group therapy with children or family therapy with whole families. Alternatively, the treatment may be indirect, when the psychologist advises parents or teachers on therapeutic programmes that can be implemented in the home or school. Children who are judged to have special educational needs may be recommended for placement in special schools or units, but they are no longer automatically transferred out of mainstream schools. Therapeutic work with children has much in common with clinical and counselling psychology, but it requires specialized skills in dealing with children and particular expertise in handling problems of educational adjustment.

Because of their skills and training, educational and school psychologists are uniquely qualified to perform evaluation research designed to establish the effectiveness of educational policies and teaching programmes in particular schools or school systems. For example, a school that has been running a remedial reading programme may enlist the methodological, statistical, and assessment skills of an educational psychologist to reach a verdict on its effectiveness and to offer advice as to how it might be improved.

Three controversies within the profession of educational or school psychology are worth mentioning briefly. The first revolves around access to records. Some educational or school psychologists believe that records should be confidential, while others believe that teachers, parents, and even the children to whom they relate, provided they are old enough to understand them, should be given access to them. The second controversy concerns the issue of labelling. Some educational or school psychologists see it as one of their chief functions to give appropriate names to the problems that they diagnose, whereas others believe that labelling is apt to have harmful effects on children and that it is more helpful to describe children in terms of their strengths and weaknesses. The third controversy arises from the question *Who are the clients?* Some educational or school psychologists consider the children with whom they work to be their clients, while others consider the schoolteachers and parents who refer the children to them to be their clients.

To register as a Chartered Educational Psychologist in England, Wales, or Northern Ireland you need an honours degree in psychology accredited by the BPS, a teaching qualification, a minimum of two years' teaching experience, and a master's degree or professional training qualification in educational psychology that usually takes one year to complete, followed by a year's practice as an educational psychologist under the supervision of a Chartered Psychologist. The order in which these qualifications are obtained may vary. Educational psychologists in Scotland do not require teaching experience. Competition for places on accredited professional training courses in educational psychology is quite keen, in spite of the long training, and a good first degree plus some relevant work experience is usually needed to secure a place.

Occupational and industrial/organizational psychology

Occupational or industrial/organizational (I/O) psychologists are concerned with problems related to people in work and unemployment. They are employed in business and industry, government agencies, and private practice. Most occupational psychologists in the United Kingdom are employed by government agencies such as the Civil Service, the Department of Employment and the Manpower Services Commission, the Ministry of Defence, and the Department of the Environment. Others are employed by private companies and consultancy firms, and a few work independently as management consultants. Some people nowadays call this profession work psychology.

Some of the problems with which occupational or I/O psychologists deal are vocational guidance and selection, problems of work motivation and job satisfaction, absenteeism in organizations, improvement of communication within organizations, design and implementation of training courses, teaching of social and human relations skills, improvement of promotion structures, evaluation of job performance, and problems of safety and welfare. They also counsel individual employees about career development or retraining following redundancy or retirement. In general, they are concerned with all aspects of the well-being and efficiency of people in work and with psychological aspects of unemployment. The three most important branches of occupational or I/O psychology are personnel psychology, ergonomics or human factors psychology, and organizational psychology, and I shall comment briefly on each of these in turn.

Personnel psychology includes job analysis, personnel selection and placement, and training of employees in industry. An occupational psychologist usually begins a job analysis by producing a job description, in the form of a detailed description of the work normally done by a person carrying out the job. The next step is the construction of a job specification, describing what a person in the job ought ideally to do. The final step is the specification of a set of job requirements, consisting of a list of the skills and training needed by a person to perform the job satisfactorily. The list of job requirements may be viewed as a distillation of the personal factors that are important in carrying out the work. Job analysis is used in many branches of personnel work, including selection and placement of employees and evaluation of employee productivity for purposes of promotion. A job analysis can be a helpful guide for recruiters, a basis upon which screening tests for applicants can be devised, and a starting-point for instructors who wish to develop job training programmes for employees.

Most personnel psychologists spend a great deal of their time on employee selection and placement, and it is obviously in the interests of both employers and employees that people should be recruited into jobs that are best suited to their individual aptitudes and interests. Personnel selection and placement became firmly established during the Second World War, when research showed that carefully constructed psychometric tests could successfully identify people most likely to succeed as aircraft pilots, navigators, bombardiers, or other skilled members of the armed services.

The class of tests most often used by personnel psychologists are those designed to measure specific aptitudes and abilities. Research has suggested that five groups of aptitudes and abilities account, singly or in various combinations, for success in a wide range of jobs. They are the following: verbal ability, spatial visualization, numerical ability, perceptual speed and accuracy, and psychomotor ability (including manual dexterity). Reliable and valid tests have been devised for measuring these qualities, and they are widely used in personnel work. Equally useful for certain kinds of jobs are tests of interests and personality. Research has shown that such personal characteristics can be evaluated much more accurately by objective tests than by subjective methods such as interviews.

Various factors have to be borne in mind when test results, together with employee records and references, are used for selecting employees and placing them in particular positions. In particular, the relative costs of two different kinds of selection and placement errors, called false positives and false negatives, have to be weighed against each other. For example, in selecting astronauts, the consequences of false positives (incorrect predictions that certain candidates will succeed at the job) are likely to be much more costly than false negatives (incorrect predictions that certain candidates will turn out to be unsuitable). In selecting trainee computer programmers, on the other hand, the reverse may apply, because false positives may not matter very much and the primary objective may be to avoid false negatives that entail overlooking potentially able candidates.

Personnel psychologists are sometimes involved in devising, implementing, and evaluating training methods. Many different techniques of training are used, including on-the-job coaching, demonstrations, simulations (used in training aircraft pilots and air traffic controllers, for example), lectures, printed instruction manuals, films, and programmed or computer-administered instruction. The optimal combination of training techniques for a particular job depends on considerations of time, expense, and effectiveness, and personnel psychologists often have to evaluate these factors in order to devise the best training programmes in specific cases.

Ergonomics, called human factors psychology or engineering psychology in the United States, differs from personnel psychology in so far as it is concerned with fitting jobs to people rather than people to jobs. Ergonomists design jobs, equipment, and work places to maximize performance and well-being and to minimize accidents, fatigue, boredom, and energy expenditure. This branch of occupational psychology rests heavily on the findings of basic research in the areas of sensation and perception, cognition, and learning and skills (see chapter 3).

Ergonomics has yielded important contributions to psychological aspects of equipment design. During the Second World War, the development of extremely complicated machines controlled by human operators, such as advanced military aircraft, led to research into the design of optimal human–machine interfaces. Early work in this area focused on finding the best ways of arranging controls and instrument panels. This form of "knobs and dials" psychology led to significant improvements in equipment design. For example, one type of improvement arose from the discovery of population stereotypes regarding the ways in which people (often unconsciously) expect controls to function. Simple examples of population stereotypes are the following. Most people unconsciously expect a knob on an electrical appliance to increase the output when it is turned clockwise and to decrease the output when it is turned anticlockwise, but we expect a water or gas tap to function in exactly the opposite way, decreasing the flow when it is turned clockwise and increasing the flow when it is turned anticlockwise. Controls that do not function in the expected ways cause irritation, inefficiency, and operator errors. Ergonomists have discovered a great deal about how to design equipment so as to make work efficient and comfortable. The information technology revolution of the 1980s and 1990s generated intensive research into the optimal design of keyboards, programming languages, and visual display units.

Ergonomists have also devoted attention to the effects of fatigue, boredom, and noise on human performance. As industrial processes become more automated, an increasing number of jobs entail passive monitoring of computer screens. The performance of such jobs requires long periods of continuous alertness and vigilance. Research into these aspects of human performance has led to many important findings that have been applied to the design of such jobs.

The British postcode illustrates the application of experimental research to a familiar problem of ergonomics. The following three findings from the laboratories of experimental psychologists underlie the postcode. First, strings of letters or digits are remembered and copied more quickly and accurately if they are presented

in groups of three than in any other way. Second, digits are easier to remember and copy than letters, partly because there are only ten different digits but twenty-six different letters. Third, items in the middle of strings are more likely to be forgotten and copied inaccurately than those at the beginnings and ends. On the recommendations of psychologists, these findings were incorporated into the design of the British postcode as follows. The standard postcode consists of six characters, in two groups of three. They are not all digits, because that would provide only a million distinct addresses, and this was considered insufficient for the purposes of the Post Office, but six letters would provide more combinations than are necessary. Therefore, the standard postcode consists of four letters and two digits, and the digits are placed in the middle of the string, where errors are most likely. For example, the postcode of the British Psychological Society is LE1 7DR. The result is a system that maximizes the speed and accuracy of addressing and sorting mail.

Organizational psychology focuses on the structures and functions of organizations and the activities of the people within them. It is applied not only in industrial organizations, but also in schools, hospitals, prisons, military units, and other non-industrial organizations. It draws heavily on the findings of basic research into learning and skills, motivation and emotion, and individual differences and personality (see chapter 3).

One important aspect of organizational psychology concerns job satisfaction, employee attitudes and motivation, and their effects on absenteeism, labour turnover, and organizational productivity and efficiency. Evidence from applied research in this area has revealed that job satisfaction depends mainly on five factors: the nature of the work itself, wages and salaries, attitudes towards supervisors, relations with co-workers, and opportunities for promotion. A scale called the Job Descriptive Index is sometimes used by organizational psychologists to measure job satisfaction on these five factors. Job satisfaction depends less than most people realize on the *absolute* levels of satisfaction and more on the discrepancy between employee expectations and experience on the job. When experience in a job fails to live up to expectations, job satisfaction tends to be low, although the same work might produce quite high levels of job satisfaction among employees with more realistic expectations. Of course, employees form their expectations mainly by comparing their jobs with those of others. Organizational psychologists believe that it is in the interests of management to ensure that prospective employees are given realistic information about jobs rather than being misled into expecting more than the jobs can offer. Although low job satisfaction leads to high absenteeism and labour turnover, the relationship between job satisfaction and productivity is not straightforward.

In the United Kingdom, a Chartered Occupational Psychologist requires a good first degree in psychology accredited by the BPS plus a one-year BPS-accredited professional training course in occupational, industrial/organizational, or applied psychology, followed by two years' practice under the supervision of a Chartered Psychologist. Alternatively, prospective occupational psychologists may sit a BPS examination called the Postgraduate Certificate in Occupational Psychology, after which they must work under supervision for a minimum of three years.

Forensic and criminological psychology

Forensic and criminological psychologists work in penal institutions, act as consultants to lawyers or the police, testify as expert witnesses in court, and work with ex-offenders in the community. In England and Wales, psychologists are employed in over a hundred different types of penal institutions within the Home Office Prison Department, including prisons, youth custody centres or young offender institutions, and remand centres, and they also work in special hospitals and regional secure units within the National Health Service. Forensic and criminological psychology draws to some extent on research in the areas of abnormal and social psychology (see chapter 3). The terminology in this field has become slightly loose and confused, but roughly speaking forensic psychology deals with psychological aspects of criminal investigation and legal processes in courts of law, and criminological psychology deals with psychological aspects of criminal behaviour.

Criminological psychology includes diagnostic assessment of prison inmates with psychological disturbances such as antisocial personality disorder, uncontrollable anger, depression, sleep disorders, loss of identity, lack of assertiveness, guilt feelings, and other psychological disturbances. Criminological psychologists sometimes implement individual and group therapy with psychologically disturbed inmates, develop inmate classification schemes, and carry out research into aspects of operational performance and the movement and treatment of prisoners. They are often responsible for staff training, including the design, implementation, and evaluation of training courses on interview techniques and methods of dealing with hostage-taking incidents, and pre-release social skills training programmes for prisoners. Criminological psychologists work closely with prison staff members, medical practitioners, and probation officers.

In England and Wales, the first one or two years of employment as a criminological psychologist are normally regarded as an in-service training period. During this training phase, a newly recruited criminological psychologist normally works under the close supervision of a more senior colleague gaining experience in testing, interviewing, research methodology, and report-writing.

A branch of forensic and criminological psychology that made rapid advances during the 1990s is investigative psychology. Investigative psychologists work closely with the police in applying psychological principles to the investigation of crimes and the apprehension of serious criminals, especially serial murderers and rapists. The pattern of behaviour of serial criminals often enables an investigative psychologist to develop a criminal profile of the probable characteristics of the perpetrator, and there are cases in which this has led to the arrest of serious offenders.

In the United Kingdom, Chartered Forensic Psychologists who work in special hospitals and regional secure units within the National Health Service have usually first qualified as clinical psychologists. Prison psychologists in England and Wales require a first degree in psychology accredited by the BPS, after which they must pass a selection procedure run by the Civil Service in order to obtain posts as Basic Grade Psychologists in the prison service. There are no positions for criminological psychologists in penal institutions in Scotland or Northern Ireland. Psychological work in penal institutions in those parts of the United Kingdom is carried out by clinical psychologists employed by the National Health Service. In the United States, there are many postgraduate training courses in forensic and criminological psychology, and in the

United Kingdom such courses began to spring up in universities in the 1990s.

Other openings

Apart from the major professions of psychology, there are many other employment prospects for psychology graduates. The emerging area of health psychology, which is concerned with psychological aspects of health promotion and the prevention and treatment of illness, provides work for psychologists in hospitals, medical schools, rehabilitation centres, health research units, and health authorities. Health psychologists design and implement programmes to help people lose weight, give up smoking, manage stress, and stay fit. An example of research in health psychology involving psychological factors in breast cancer was discussed in chapter 4 in connection with quasi-experimental designs. Sports psychology, concerned with psychological factors associated with athletic performance, is also emerging as an active field of applied psychology and is providing career opportunities in educational institutions and sports clubs. A psychology degree also provides an excellent basis for a career in market research, advertising, social work, nursing, personnel management, and various specialized forms of therapy including art therapy, music therapy, and psycho-analysis, each of which has its own training requirements.

How to become a psychologist

Now that you have read this book almost to the end, you should have a reasonably sound understanding of the nature and subject matter of psychology, its aims, research methods, and historical development, and the range of professions and career opportunities that are open to properly qualified psychologists. Perhaps you picked this book up because you were intrigued to find out something about psychology but have now come to the conclusion that psychology is definitely not for you. In that case the book has succeeded in curing your misconceptions relatively painlessly and inexpensively. Alternatively, you may now be sufficiently attracted by the subject to want to read more deeply into it, in which case the groundwork provided by this book should help you to find your bearings in the more technical literature that you will read in the future. A third possibility is that you are sufficiently inspired to consider becoming qualified and possibly pursuing a career in psychology. A few general comments about qualifications and training may therefore be helpful.

The first step on the road to becoming a qualified psychologist is the satisfactory completion of secondary schooling. The basic qualification for any career in psychology is a recognized honours degree, and admission into degree courses usually depends on secondary school examination results. In the United Kingdom, the minimum requirement is usually two A level passes and in most cases GCSE mathematics, but competition for places on undergraduate courses is fairly stiff and two bare passes may be insufficient to gain admission. The formal entry requirements are sometimes waived for mature applicants who are over 23 years old. Although psychology is available as a school subject, applicants who have studied it at school are not at a great advantage in applying for places on degree courses. Other suitable school subjects for intending psychology students include biology, mathematics, economics, English, and history, but most admissions tutors are more concerned with the grades than with the subjects in which they were obtained. It is sometimes easier to get a place on joint or combined honours degree courses in which psychology is read in conjunction with one or more other subjects. Some such joint and combined honours degrees are recognized by the British Psychological Society (BPS) as conferring the Graduate Basis for Registration as a Chartered Psychologist, and the Graduate Basis for Registration is a necessary prerequisite for entry into most postgraduate professional training courses and for becoming a Chartered Psychologist. Conversion courses are available at some institutions for graduates in other subjects who want to become psychologists. Psychology can be studied part-time at the Open University, and provided that certain courses are taken at honours degree level, graduates attain the Graduate Basis for Registration. A few part-time and sandwich courses are available elsewhere.

During the three or four years of study towards a first degree, a student is expected to master the basic concepts, theories, and research findings in all major areas of psychology, and to acquire a number of skills. The range of topics covered in an undergraduate syllabus comes as a surprise to many students, but readers of this book will have a good idea of what to expect. Teaching methods usually include lectures, tutorials, seminars, and laboratory classes, and towards the end of the course students are often required to carry out research projects which count towards their degree classes. Assessment schemes vary from one institution to the next but are usually based on a combination of examination results and marks received for laboratory reports, essays, and projects. Some degree courses emphasize one particular aspect of psychology such as social psychology or applied psychology. Practical work with animals is part of some undergraduate courses but not others. People who have strong ethical objections to animal research should enquire from the institutions to which they are considering applying whether they will be required to do practical work with animals.

A first degree does not, on its own, qualify a person to practise in all fields of psychology, in fact most careers in psychology require postgraduate training. I have given an outline of the requirements for the major psychological professions of clinical, educational, occupational, and criminological psychology, as well as teaching and research in psychology. Further details can be found in the publications listed below.

Further reading

For readers in the United Kingdom, The British Psychological Society (St Andrews House, 48 Princess Road East, Leicester LE1 7DR) publishes a very useful booklet for people considering studying psychology called *How about psychology? A guide to courses and careers* (3rd ed., Leicester: The British Psychological Society, 1994) and a careers booklet for people with degrees in psychology entitled *Careers in psychology: A guide to courses and opportunities in psychology* (Leicester: The British Psychological Society, 1996). More detailed information about the professions of psychology in the United Kingdom is contained in the *Professional psychology handbook* (Leicester: The British Psychological Society, 1995) and in Stephen E. Newstead's *Putting psychology to work* (2nd ed., Leicester: The British Psychological Society, 1994).

For readers in the United States, the American Psychological Association (750 First Street, NE, Washington, DC 20002) has published *Psychology/careers for the twenty-first century: Scientific problem solvers* (Washington, DC: American Psychological Journal, 1996), a little booklet that will be of help to students who are planning to take higher degrees in psychology. Drew Appleby's *The handbook of psychology* (New York: Longman, 1997) offers practical suggestions for developing critical skills and finding employment in the United States with only a first degree in psychology. A useful article on careers in the United States for psychologists with first degrees in psychology only, entitled "Careers in Psychology: Or What Can I do With a Bachelor's Degree?" by J.L. Carroll, J.L. Shmidt, and R. Sorenson can be found in the journal *Psychological Reports* (Volume 71, pp. 1151–1154, 1992).

Readers in Australia should consult the College of Psychological Practice's book *Realistic careers in psychology* (St Leonards, NSW: College of Psychological Practice, 1995).

There are many sites on the World Wide Web that provide useful and up-to-date information about the professions of psychology. Among the most worthwhile are the home pages of the American Psychological Association (http://www.apa.org/) and the British Psychological Society (http://www.bps.org.uk/), both of which contain information about a vast number of other web sites of relevance to psychology. Particularly useful for careers information in the United States is Marky Lloyd's Careers In Psychology Page (http://www.psywww.com/careers/index.htm). A useful starting point for resources and information about psychology for students and professionals is provided by PsycSite (http://stange.simplenet.com/psycsite/). Another useful guide to psychological information can be found at http://psych.hanover.edu/Krantz/lists.html. One of the most popular Internet sites for psychology-related information is Psych Web (http://www.psychwww.com/).

Index